GUIDING THE GIFTED CHILD

A PRACTICAL SOURCE FOR PARENTS AND TEACHERS

JAMES T. WEBB, PH.D.
ELIZABETH A. MECKSTROTH, M.S.
AND
STEPHANIE S. TOLAN, M.A.

Gifted Psychology Press
Scottsdale, Arizona

Published by
Great Potential Press, Inc.
(Formerly Gifted Psychology Press, Inc.)
P.O. Box 5057
Scottsdale, AZ 85261
www.giftedbooks.com

Published by
Great Potential Press, Inc.
(Formerly Gifted Psychology Press, Inc.)
P.O. Box 5057
Scottsdale, AZ 85261
www.giftedbooks.com

Formerly
Ohio Psychology Press
P.O. Box 90095
Dayton, OH 45490

copyright © 1994 by Ohio Psychology Press

Library of Congress Cataloging-in-Publication Data

Webb, James T.
 * Guiding The Gifted Child: A Practical Source for Parents and
    Teachers/James T. Webb, Elizabeth A. Meckstroth and Stephanie S. Tolan
        p.   Cm.
    Includes bibliographical references (p.   ) and index
    ISBN 0-910707-00-6 (pbk.)
    1. Gifted children -- United States.   2 Gifted children -- Education --
    United States   3.Parent and child -- United States.

    CIP 82-099939

ISBN 0-910707-00-6
Twenty Second Printing, 2002

CONTENTS

"Flowing with, rather than
fighting against . . ."

This work is dedicated to cherishing the emotional growth of all unique children, for they can deeply enrich our lives. We honor those who share a child's zest and quest for greater understanding by caring enough to read this material. We hope to offer enjoyment, support and courage that nurtures growth toward cooperatively meeting their own needs.

PREFACE

The suicide of bright, talented, 17 year old Dallas Egbert in 1980 led his parents to inquire about programs designed to meet emotional needs of gifted children and their families. It soon became apparent that such programs rarely existed, even though the need for such services seemed clear. Prompted by their quest and by their contact with us, we began a program. The intent has been to increase the awareness of parents, teachers and others working with gifted children particularly to recognize that these children and their families have special emotional needs and opportunities that are quite often overlooked and, thus, neglected. Most often this neglect results "only" in unfulfilled potential and missed enjoyments — but sometimes it leads blatantly to misery and depression. Loving our children just is not enough. As in other jobs that require management roles, we have to know what we are doing!

On the Phil Donahue show in January, 1981, Dr. and Mrs. Egbert, Dr. James Webb and others discussed these emotional needs. Responses from over 20,000 persons across the country confirmed the extent of neglect, lack of understanding, and the prevailing myths regarding gifted children and their families. Through the courtesy of Joyce Juntune (who also appeared on this Donahue show) most of these letters went to the headquarters of the National Association for Gifted Children, and

i

were answered by her. Ms. Juntune, who is the Executive Director of NAGC, continues to give valued advice and support concerning our fledgling program.

Early in 1981, we began to implement a modest program to meet some of the emotional needs of gifted children and their families. Assistance was provided by the Dallas Egbert Fund established by the Egbert family at the Wright State University Foundation in Dayton, Ohio, and by the School of Professional Psychology at Wright State University which generously opened doors to inaugurate this effort. With community cooperation, a developing program was established.

What have we done? One aspect of the program involves formal intellectual and personality assessment and intensive treatment by psychologists at the Wright State University School of Professional Psychology who consult individually with the gifted children and their families.

Another aspect provides consultation to psychologists, teachers and other professionals individually and through workshops. We have responded to numerous inquiries from professionals throughout the country who seek assistance in nurturing the emotional development of gifted children and their families. It has become apparent that professionals lack useful training on this subject.

Foremost, we are working directly with parent groups through a series of guided discussions. The series consists of ten major topics that are of concern to the gifted child's family. Generally, one topic is discussed in each session. We provide some basic written material noting key points relevant to the topic, encourage parents to share their common concerns, and offer professional comment, advice, discussion, and guidance. Through this approach, parents can share ideas and experiences, and learn from each other how to appreciate and encourage each child. They can anticipate problems and find solutions, and, we hope, prevent difficulties from occurring. Parenting requires skills that few of us are trained for or practiced at. Raising one or more gifted children can be even more demanding. As one parent noted, "Gifted children really don't change your life style; they destroy it!"

In the parents' group meetings, we have probably learned as much from the parents as they learned from us. We are deeply indebted to them for their sharing, courage and support. We all are learning to flow with, rather than fight against, a child's special abilities. Parents' comments about needs in their own families have contributed to developing this handbook. They join in our effort to help other parents and persons involved closely with gifted children.

Perhaps these pages will prompt others to establish similar parent groups elsewhere. Such parent groups could be a valuable addition to any gifted program. When gifted and enrichment classes do not exist or where they may be curtailed due to fiscal cutbacks within the educational systems, then programs for nurturing parent techniques become particularly crucial.

This book has five sections. Chapter I gives an overview of giftedness along with underlying myths and stereotypes that exist about gifted children. When some of the behaviors of these children are explored, it becomes apparent that they often are out of step with others and even within themselves. We lay groundwork for steps that can be taken to encourage self-esteem, self-respect and a strong self-identity. The concepts may help parents anticipate, prevent or inoculate their children against many of the particular stresses that they are likely to encounter.

The second section, Chapters II through XII, focuses more specifically on characteristics, on frequently occurring problems, *and* on particular suggestions for modifying behaviors. Where possible, we suggest ways of building on the strengths of gifted children, and attempt to view matters from a family point of view.

The third section, Chapter XIII, is an open letter to parents and teachers of gifted children. Written by the mother of an exceptionally gifted child, this open letter gives a real life perspective of many of the grins and groans such parents experience. Through this letter we hope you will be able to see in concrete terms many examples of the concepts presented earlier in the book.

The fourth section, Chapter XIV, is an annotated bibliography of some resources that we recommend to help increase your understanding and skills in guiding gifted children. Different books are appropriate for parents of children of different ages and in different situations. No one book has all the answers. But if you can get one or two useful ideas for nurturing from an hour or so of reading, then that time has been invested wisely! Some of these books are just basic to good parenting; others are specifically oriented to gifted and talented children.

The final section, Chapter XV, presents a list of organizations which work side by side with parents. Parent advocacy and support groups can be effective agents for system change and for individual solace. Since programs for gifted children and their families are continually evolving, coordinating organizations need updated information about your group involvement. All of you are needed in this network.

We hope you will find the contents helpful. Our attempt has been to help in a practical, rather than theoretical, way. It is our impression that there is a lack of relevant resources that provide specific behavioral suggestions. We have tried to offer a wide range of practical solutions that might answer, "So now what do we do?" Perhaps you may have other suggestions. If so, please let us hear from you. Our goal is to help gifted children and their families not only obtain extensive knowledge, but also to find understanding and peace for themselves and others in ways that facilitate their being what is most worthwhile for themselves, others, and their world.

* * * * *

"There is a great difference between knowing and understanding; you can know a lot about something and not really understand it."

Charles F. Kettering

"These children are like plants that need stakes to grow against, with gentle ties where necessary to support their natural growth, instead of being rigidly espaliered to a stone wall in artificial designs someone else devised."

Stephanie Tolan

CHAPTER I

WE DON'T HAVE A PROBLEM HERE!
. . . OR DO WE?

Recently, a nine year old girl was asked how a submarine and fish were different. After a moment she replied, "A submarine has lettuce, tomato and mayonnaise, but a fish only has tartar sauce." There are myriad stories which illustrate that gifted children often think differently from other children their age. On the one hand, this trait is delightful and surprising; but on the other hand, creative thinking may generate misunderstandings or problems for the gifted child and his or her family.

Our educational system has often generated mediocrity except for gifted athletes. From kindergarten, children are bombarded with pressures that urge them to modify their behavior and intellectual development toward the average of the group. Gifted children throughout our society may be trapped in an intellectual wasteland — a world that can be cruel to the gifted (Garfield, 1980).

Services to gifted and talented children are viewed as a low priority at federal, state and most levels of government, and by educational administrations. Even where there are legal or administrative mandates for providing services, the lack of trained personnel and funds cause programs for gifted children to be miniscule. In the years 1975-1980 federal expenditures for handicapped children were 200 times greater than those for gifted children (Lyon, 1981). The 1979 federal budget provided "more than $1,000 for each learning disabled American child versus only $2.42 per gifted and talented child. . . . In other words, more than one billion dollars for the eight to ten million disabled versus less than seven million dollars for the 2.6 million children estimated to be gifted and talented." (Lipper, 1979).

Existing services to the gifted and talented do not reach significant numbers of people, particularly the handicapped, minorities or other disadvantaged people. In minority groups the social and educational environments have "every configuration calculated to stifle potential talent." (Marland Report, 1972).

The lack of understanding and the lack of priority given by our society to these persons foster a climate in which the emotional needs of gifted children are neglected. As stated in the Marland Report (1972) of the U.S. Department of Education, "Gifted and talented children are, in fact, deprived and can suffer psychological damage and permanent impairment of their abilities to function well. . . ."

In this chapter we sketch a framework of some of the emotional needs of these children. At the same time we recognize that there are ways of using the special abilities of gifted children to help them meet their own needs, and have attempted to focus on these positive characteristics. We also have emphasized the family as a whole. We believe that the emotional well-being of the child cannot be understood without considering his family, and that the family cannot function well without understanding the emotional needs of the gifted child.

Defining Giftedness

What is a gifted child? Is there more than one kind of giftedness? Is giftedness the same thing as genius? Are all gifted children about the same in their intellectual ability? What are the criteria for defining giftedness, and what are the distinguishing characteristics? When a child is gifted, does she[1] just think faster or is she different in the way she thinks? Is being talented the same thing as being gifted?

Such questions illustrate the difficulties in defining exactly what is meant by giftedness. After considerable study, the Marland Report (1972) concluded that six major categories of gifted and talented children should be recognized since each category contained children "... who by virtue of outstanding abilities are capable of high performance." The children included were those with demonstrated achievement and/or potential in any of the following areas:

1. General intellectual ability
2. Specific academic aptitude
3. Creative or productive thinking
4. Leadership ability
5. Visual or performing arts
6. Psychomotor ability

Although psychomotor ability (e.g. athletics) has since been deleted, these categories encompass a wide range of giftedness that extends beyond a simple notion of intelligence. In practice, however, most programs for gifted children emphasize the first two categories with a focus on intellectual ability and academic aptitude (Fox, 1981). Children with specific talents such as art or music but lacking a measured high level of intelligence usually are neglected and fall through the cracks. If they can afford it, their parents buy private enrichment.

Children identified as gifted typically have mental abilities in the upper two and one-half to three percent of the population. This does *not* mean that two or three out of every 100 persons are geniuses. They *are* gifted. Only a fraction of *gifted* are geniuses.

How unusual are gifted persons and geniuses in our general population? Figure 1 shows the distribution of mental abilities as measured by tests of intelligence. Although test scores are not

---

[1]For simplicity, we have chosen to alternate "he" and "she" in our examples.

the only way of measuring giftedness, we will use IQ scores as a convenient way to explain such points.

The average IQ score is 100. The shaded area on the extreme right in Figure 1 indicates the percentage most often used to define "gifted." Although an IQ score of 130 or above is generally used as a cut-off score, various professionals and school systems may use different scores such as an IQ of 125 along with other indications of creativity or talent.

An IQ score of 130 may have more meaning if it is put in a different perspective. The average IQ score for persons graduating from college is about 120; for executives, scientists and physicians, about 130. About half of these scientists and physicians have IQ scores less than 130 (Cronbach, 1960). A person with an IQ above 130 is potentially capable of succeeding in almost any occupation or pursuit.

As shown in Figure 1, most tests of intelligence only measure an IQ score as high as 145 to 160, though it is possible to extrapolate scores beyond this. Intelligence has no absolute ceiling; no one knows how high intelligence could be. Some people have IQ scores estimated to be as high as 180 or even 200. Though several formal definitions exist, usually people with above 160 IQ are the ones called geniuses.

How Many "Gifted" Are There?

Figure 2 shows graphically the proportion of persons considered gifted and their actual numbers among America's 226 million inhabitants.

About five million persons in the United States are gifted, with less than one million of these being "exceptionally gifted." The numbers get even smaller as we go above an IQ score of 140. Only about 7,200 persons have IQ scores above 160. Fewer than 120 have scores of 180 or above — extremely rare.

Figure 1
Distribution of Intelligence Quotients

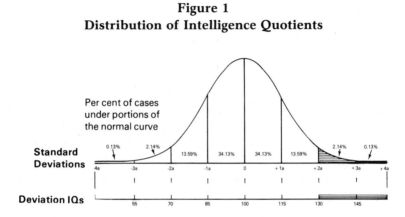

Per cent of cases under portions of the normal curve

Figure 2
How Many Gifted Are There?
(Based on U.S. Population of 226,000,000)

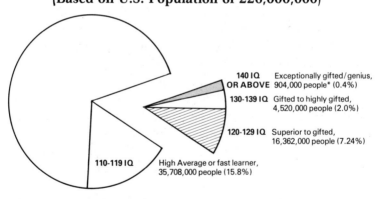

140 IQ OR ABOVE — Exceptionally gifted/genius, 904,000 people* (0.4%)

130-139 IQ — Gifted to highly gifted, 4,520,000 people (2.0%)

120-129 IQ — Superior to gifted, 16,362,000 people (7.24%)

110-119 IQ — High Average or fast learner, 35,708,000 people (15.8%)

*Ratio of highly gifted to general population

1 out of 260 individuals may have an IQ of 140 or above
1 out of 2,330 individuals may have an IQ of 150 or above
1 out of 31,560 individuals may have an IQ of 160 or above
1 out of 652,600 individuals may have an IQ of 170 or above
1 out of 2,000,000 individuals may have an IQ of 180 or above

Gifted persons are a diverse group. At the lower end of the gifted range is an IQ score of 130; the upper score is approximately 200 — a spread of 70 points. Consider that there is only a 45 point range between the *Borderline Mentally Retarded* (IQ of 85) and the *Very Superior* (IQ of 130). A further consideration is that the two-thirds of *all* people have IQ scores in the range from 90 to 110 — a spread of only 20 IQ points. It is not appropriate to think that all gifted are alike. In particular, "exceptionally gifted" persons (IQ 140 and above), although they are a minority, exhibit a wider range of abilities than do the remaining gifted (IQ 130-140) who are more commonly encountered.

Identifying Gifted Children

The IQ score is just one way to identify a gifted child. Other measurements include: school achievement, creative behaviors, and teacher and parent evaluations. IQ scores are only a single statement of a person's overall potential. A person can be gifted in a creative sense without having an IQ score above 130. Also, these measures of mental ability called "IQ" are not absolute. They may vary from one testing session to another by 5, 10 or even 20 IQ score points depending on numerous factors. Some of these influencing factors are rapport with the psychologist, distracting noises outside the testing room, or the child's general well-being. A child who is tense or hungry or has a headache will not perform as well as one who is relaxed and feeling good.

Further, an IQ score is a composite of several different aspects of "intelligence." Some children are gifted in language and verbal areas — others in music or in the arts. Some have exceptional abilities in visual or spatial relationships such as architecture or mechanical design. These children may or may not be gifted in language usage. Such variations appear to be related to "right brain" or "left brain" differences recently described by Kane and Kane (1979).

Despite imperfections, current tests of intelligence and creativity are helpful and important instruments for measuring one child's intellectual abilities as compared with those of others of the same age. To some extent, such comparisons occur in every classroom as teachers develop expectations of childrens' potential to learn based on their observations and grading.

Making realistic judgments is as difficult for teachers as it is for parents. Studies have shown that teachers are unable to identify over half of the children determined as gifted by individual intelligence tests (Fox, 1981).

It appears that identifying gifted children through classroom abilities and the measurement of intelligence through group administered intelligence tests are both limited since the child must be both willing and able to reveal his giftedness in the ordinary, expected ways. It may be this factor, in addition to the apathy, indifference and ignorance of professionals, that accounts for the low recognition of gifted children by school administrators. One national survey summarized in the Marland Report (1972) revealed that 57.5% of administrators in U.S. schools believed that they had *no* gifted pupils. This same survey further showed that even when they were recognized as gifted, one-third of these students were given no special instruction. The remaining two-thirds largely received only token assistance.

Parents often are the first to recognize a child's giftedness. Parents have some idea quite early in the child's life that he is advanced compared to others of the same age. One mother identified her 3 year old's curiosity and thinking ability by saying "she drives me crazy at the mall with all her questions and her energy!" Sometimes an early and unusual sense of humor is evident, such as one girl who asked her mother if that was an "itchy cake" — that is, one from "scratch". Although children's

developmental lags and spurts make comparison difficult, guidelines for standards of developmental behaviors are available
(Tannenbaum & Neuman, 1980). While parents must be aware
of natural pride and a possible tendency to think their own
children are bound to be gifted, they also need to trust their own
observations and judgment about their child's abilities.

Giftedness That Doesn't Blossom

Perhaps you have decided you have a gifted child. That means
she will grow up to be a responsible, contributing and valued
member of society, right? Doctor, lawyer, scientist, poet, president! Not necessarily! The prestigious Marland Report (1972)
noted that "disturbingly, research has confirmed that many
talented children perform far below their intellectual potential.
We are increasingly being stripped of the comfortable notion
that a bright mind will make its own way." In 1975, one report
(Lemov, 1979), estimated that as many as 15-30% of high school
dropouts are gifted and talented. Other studies have shown that
most youngsters identified as intellectually gifted were significantly underachieving. Depression appears common among
gifted persons, and there is even some suggestion that suicides
appear to be increasing among this group of teenagers.

Why do some persons with high potential fail to live up to it?
Why do some take their own lives? What could an intellectually
gifted person possibly be so desperately unhappy about? How
could high mental abilities cause problems for a child or a
family?

More Is Not Necessarily Better

There are many underlying myths about gifted children. In the
early 1900s the prevalent myth was "early ripe . . . early rot."

That is, a child who bloomed early in life supposedly would wither and die at a young age, or at least develop a sudden post-adolescent stupidity. This simple-minded generalization has been replaced by more recent misconceptions such as those shown in Table 1.

Table 1

Some Underlying Myths About Gifted Children

Myths common in public perception:
  They have everything going their way.
  They can suceed without help.
  Their special abilities are always prized by their families.
  They should be valued primarily for their brain power.
  They are more stable and mature emotionally.
  They have gotten "something for nothing."
  They naturally want to be social isolates.
 	
Myths common among parents and educators:
  They are not aware of being different unless someone tells them they are.
  They will reveal their giftedness.
  Their giftedness needs to be emphasized above all else.
  They need constant challenge by others if they are to achieve.
  They need to be disciplined more than other children.
  They should assume extra responsibility for others.
  They enjoy serving as "examples" for other children.

Unfortunately many parents, educators, and policy-makers in our society appear to be unaware that their behavior is influenced by these false assumptions. Too often school administrators' apathy has hurt. They may make statements like, "There isn't any problem here in our district! These kids can take care of themselves." "All they need is a little extra work to challenge them." "If only I'd had what they have, I'd be rich, famous, or both." "Why should we do extra for those who already have everything going for them?"

Contrary to what most people believe, a gifted mind is not necessarily able to find its own way. Although gifted students possess exceptional capabilities, most cannot excel without assistance. They need assistance academically, but they also need assistance emotionally through understanding, acceptance, support and encouragement. Even in reports of the famous long-term Terman studies (Coleman, 1980), underachievers are often overlooked. Follow-up studies revealed that about 20% of these children had clear emotional problems. Their underachievement and emotional difficulties occurred even though Terman's identification and sample selection procedures served to exclude children who were likely to have personal or emotional mala-justments (Terman, 1925). Most of the Terman study children were nominated by their teachers and then were required to score high on group administered tests — procedures which would tend to favor children willing and able to display their giftedness. Gifted children who were already emotionally disturbed, unmotivated toward classroom work, or who had unusual ways of expressing their mental ability were not as likely to be included.

What Does Our Society Really Value?

Does our society really value giftedness? Perhaps in limited situations — in the "right place."

American culture tends to reinforce and support mediocrity and conformity. The emphasis is on training persons to absorb ideas passively. Human drama and problems of living are often oversimplified through TV and other media with bland ideas and obvious solutions. Our society does not greatly prize intellectual stimulation, creativity and mental diversity. We may be constantly urged to develop our bodies and our social skills, but as a society we are less enthusiastic about developing our mental potential.

It says something about our culture that in 1979 less than 30 universities in the country had graduate-level programs specifically in gifted education, and school districts were only serving slightly more than one-third of our gifted population through formal programs (Lyons, 1981). In classes across the country, only one out of six teachers of gifted classes has had any formal training for this special work (Lyons, 1981).

Where school programs for the gifted exist, too often the emphasis is only on accelerated repetition of *facts.* Some progressive programs emphasize principles, concepts, and evaluative thinking. Few reward curiosity; commonly they stress conformity. They place little emphasis on developing an understanding of the self, an ability to relate well to others, sensitivity to feelings, and a positive self-concept.

Does a person benefit by having extensive factual and theoretical knowledge if he is an emotional or social misfit, or spends his life in great personal misery? A question worth considering is where and how may gifted persons find emotional worth.

What Are Gifted Children Like?

Gifted children typically view the world in nontraditional ways; they are "divergent thinkers." They are likely to be intense in their feelings, their behavior and their views. Gifted and creative children particularly view the world through a quite different set of glasses than less gifted children. An exceptionally gifted child can be said to see the world through an electron microscope as compared with normal vision. This child sees what others do not see, and what others cannot even imagine. Consider, for example, the second grade teacher who asks the class a question such as, "Which numbers in the series 1, 2, 3, 4, 5, 6, 7 can be divided evenly by 2?" only to be answered, "All of them." Or consider the twelve year old child who enjoys developing variations in the computer enhancement of photographic images.

The thoughts and experiences that gifted children carry around in their heads typically are far more important and interesting to them than what is going on around them. Perhaps this partially explains why so many gifted children have imaginary playmates during their preschool years. Since they grew up being "gifted," these children expect that the world appears to others as it appears to them, and that other children are as intensely concerned as they. It usually comes as a surprise to them that others do not share their perspectives, their curiosity and intensity. It also surprises them that others see *them* differently than they see themselves.

Gifted children not only see things differently, they also typically try to do things in different ways, sometimes even ordinary tasks or activities. They can see many possibilities and alternative solutions within a situation. This, in itself, may cause tensions. When one two year old was told that she had to nap until the little hand was on three, she turned all knobs behind the clock until it read 3:00!

Though these children can see many possibilities, their limited experience may impair their judgment to anticipate the outcome of these possibilities. Thus, they usually engage in a great deal of experimentation, often with quite interesting, or even disastrous results. Young Tom Edison is said to have persuaded another child to jump off a roof to test an invention. Even his ever-tolerant mother lost her tolerance that time! In the classroom, curious questioning about possibilities and implications can quickly wreck a lesson plan! At home it can drive a mother at least to seek shelter in the bathroom.

While the gifted child's curiosity and experimentation may put a strain on family members, the energy and enthusiasm with which he pursues his activities can add even greater tension. Gifted children typically exhibit an unusually high level of energy and may need less sleep than anyone else in the family. It is not unusual for parents to insist on regular naptimes — so the parents can get a little rest!

Since their activity level can be so high, gifted children are sometimes misdiagnosed by parents or pediatricians as hyperactive and may even be placed on medication. Careful observation of the gifted child's activity can avoid such an error, however. While the truly hyperactive child has a very brief attention span, the gifted child can concentrate on a single task for long periods. Also, where the hyperactive child's activity is both constant and random, the gifted child's activity is usually directed to specific goals.

The usual school setting becomes boring, particularly when the child is not appropriately placed, or when the system tries to force the child into its preset average mold. Most gifted children begin school full of enthusiasm, but often lose this excitement quickly. One such child arrived one-half hour early to school "just to get things done before I get too busy." Her second grade teacher scolded her for being so early. This child learned from the event . . . but what she learned did not favor school!

Some experts have suggested that gifted elementary children may have one-fourth to one-half of their class time "left over." Exceptionally gifted children may have as much as three-fourths of their class time with little to do, and are often given busy work or are left to their own devices. In comparison to their classmates, these children increasingly depart from average grade level work as they progress through school, *if their educational program permits* (Marland, 1972). What they do with their extra time varies from child to child or from day to day. In the earlier grades they may try to help other children in the class, or help the teacher, or become "creative" . . . often to the dismay of the teacher and their classmates!

Children who do not wish to be disruptive may become creatively inattentive, and develop any number of methods for passing time. One six year old described his obvious daydreaming over his workbook as "playing in my mind." By age eight he had learned to appear to pay attention to his teacher while sorting her spoken syllables by base 2. Other children tell of counting their teeth with their tongue or teaching themselves to write backwards. From the teacher's viewpoint, a class of 28 children can be a problem when it contains one or more gifted children, and the problem may be even greater when such a child is not recognized as being gifted. Even the sympathetic and conscientious teacher in the regular classroom seldom finds time to devote to the gifted pupil.

Adults may not identify gifted children, but these children identify each other early in life. They gravitate toward each other out of mutual enjoyment. In some cases, however, there are not enough other children with similar abilities in the vicinity, particularly in economically disadvantaged areas. Where other gifted children are not available, the young gifted child becomes aware that he feels and acts differently from others. Even as a preschooler he may begin to feel left out. Unfortunately, the child does not understand *why* she is different, and may begin to feel there is something wrong with her.

Who Is a Peer for a Gifted Child?

Peer relationships often are a problem. The gifted child's interests, intellectual maturity, and play activities are in many ways more sophisticated than those of other children of the same age. He will explore ideas and issues earlier than his peers and be concerned with satisfying his own desire for knowledge and meeting challenges. A gifted child may be interested in hearing a virtuoso playing a Beethoven piano concerto, while the same age child across the street is delighted to see a man on TV play the piano with his nose.

The sophistication and advanced behavior is not, however, spread equally across all the activities and interests of a gifted child. Her manual dexterity may lag behind her level of knowledge and interests. An *intellectual* peer for the gifted child may not be the same person who is a physical peer with skill levels in baseball or hopscotch more in keeping with her age group. Thus the gifted child often needs several different kinds of peers . . . some for sports, different ones for intellectual pursuits, and still others for emotional friendships.

Sometimes by age three or four these children are already out of step with their friends. They may even be out of step within themselves since their interests and knowledge outdistance their ability to perform, particularly during their younger years. For example, the child may have an excellent sense of artistic perspective, but his fine-motor coordination may not be sufficient to allow him to draw adequately with a pencil or to cut with a pair of scissors. This discrepancy is very frustrating, and the continued inability to produce what he can imagine may lead him to quit trying altogether.

Sometimes gifted children are highly focused in their interests and seem to immerse themselves in a topic to the point of fanaticism. They may have difficulty understanding why others are not as interested as they in dinosaurs or violins or quarks. Often, particularly early in life, gifted children hop-skip intensely from interest to interest. This may cause others to view them as "disorganized" or "scattered." But even the child with broad and varied interests is intense about the subject uppermost at the moment.

A child's tendency to develop, or not to develop, her interests seems related partly to inborn temperament and partly to how inquisitiveness is handled at home and at school. If it is acceptable to be inquisitive, or even diversely scattered, the gifted child's range of interests will likely be broad. Gradual focusing will occur later as a result of guided support. If, however, the environment is not supportive, the child is more likely to retreat into limited, perhaps even unique, interests as a means of withdrawal and protection of her identity.

Most gifted children develop language abilities astoundingly early. Their large vocabularies quickly leave their peers behind and may cause communication problems. They are like the scientist who could not talk in "layman's language" because he did not speak that language! Thus, they are likely to gravitate toward adults and older children who share not only their interests but also their vocabulary. These relationships may be satisfying to the child, and may even be a source of pride to the parents. But mixed-age relationships separate the gifted child from classmates his own age, may reduce his number of friendships, and could make him seem to be trying to appear "too grown up." Being accustomed to adult company can condition a child to assume a parent role with other children, often with alienating effects.

Other problems may arise because the gifted child's social judgment and maturity do not develop at the same rate as his curiosity or knowledge about facts. For example, a gifted child may have vast knowledge about different religions from a factual point of view. She may not, however, appreciate how socially inappropriate it is to point out to Dad's boss that his religious views are illogical.

Many adults forget that the gifted child's intellectual development and emotional maturity seldom keep pace with each other.

They expect the gifted child to act as mature as he is intelligent. They do not expect him to act his age, and may even become upset when he does. The gifted child is likely to show a perplexingly diverse pattern. At times he will appear quite mature, and at other times he will seem quite childish. In the morning he wants to watch a highly technical TV program, "Genetic Transformations Within Cloning;" but that evening wants to see the horror movie, "Screaming Eyeball," or play with dolls. A boy may carry on a reasoned discussion about the possibility of nuclear holocaust and immediately afterward fight with his brother about who gets the front seat on the way to the grocery.

How Do Others React to Giftedness?

Gifted children may be generally neglected by our society, but they are rarely ignored as individuals. Their alacrity, intensity and quirks of behaviors often evoke strong emotional reactions from siblings, peers, teachers, and parents that the gifted child needs to be put in his place or taken down a peg. Too often terms such as those in Table 2 are applied to gifted children in a negative and even punishing fashion. The underlying message is "they better learn right now that they have to be just like everyone else!"

But take a minute to think about the descriptive terms in Table 2. What makes them negative is that they do not fit with *our* way of doing things! Each of these terms could also have positive meaning. For example "manipulative" could just reflect that the child is constructive and creative about getting what she wants. "Hyperactive" could mean that he is energetic and curious about many things.

Unfortunately too many adults feel that they must put the gifted child in her place by publicly criticizing her abilities, or by sarcastically implying that her giftedness is undesirable and

Table 2

Gifted Children Need to be put in their place because they are:
* * * * * * – different   – out-of-step   – manipulative – show-offs who always know the answers   – mischievous – hyperactive   – stubborn   – insensitive to others – likely to question my way of doing things – aggressive   – weird   – anti-social   – conceited – impertinent and challenging   – bossy – disrespectful   – preoccupied with themselves – not willing to do things the traditional way – undisciplined * * * * * *

a problem. They make it a liability, rather than an asset, to be gifted. A major strength of the child is turned against her, thus setting the stage for emotional withdrawal, added stress, insecurity and poor adjustment.

Gifted Children Are Emotionally Sensitive

Gifted children are emotionally intense with extra emotional antennae. This may be evident not only in their interactions with others and their attitudes toward themselves, but also in their reactions to everday events — the wonderment at the changes of fall foliage, the tears of passion upon first hearing Beethoven, the absorbed fascination with a prism of light. They see the implications and interrelations of events, and feel the emotional impact. As one mother recalled, her six year old son told her when his pet mouse died, "Mom, for a person my age, I've seen too much death!" Attitudes and emotions of others have a strong impact on gifted children. They are able, at a much earlier age than most people suspect, to interpret body language and to read the emotions conveyed in the tone of voice. Even when they cannot understand the words, they understand the feelings. Many parents, to their distress, note how often their gifted children are overly sensitive — taking a minor insult or joke too much to heart or empathizing with another child to the point that the gifted child seems to suffer even more than the victim himself.

Like most young children, gifted children want very much to be liked by others. They seek acceptance and approval; and they typically try to please through emphasizing some personal strength that is recognized by others. Often this strength is intellectual achievement and this may lead to many demonstrations of mental prowess. Parental over-emphasis on achievement can prompt perfectionism, and gifted children easily fall into the trap of being perfectionists even when they are not being pressured by others. They set high standards for themselves even when they do not have the skills to meet these standards, so what objectively is unusual achievement may be interpreted by the child as failure.

A family of a gifted child can easily drift into a pattern of rewarding performance and achievement too much, so that the mental giftedness becomes the only arrow in the child's quiver. When the aunts, uncles and grandparents come to visit, the family may get Johnny to demonstrate his mathematical abilities, or define words, or display his talent at the piano. Gifted Johnny may get the notion that if he cannot produce results, he is not worth very much, and that he is only valued for his giftedness. More than one gifted child has indicated to us that he was made to feel lazy and self-indulgent when he was not "at work," or when he was playing with peers who "can't teach you anything." Other parents may know better than to push performance, but may nonetheless give their child the impression that his giftedness is his primary or only asset. Some parents adopt a *prima donna* attitude where they excuse their child from having to do ordinary tasks because "He's gifted!"

For all too many gifted children, self-concept rests heavily, if not entirely, upon being "gifted" and on accomplishments. It is precarious for any person to hang her self-concept on only one hook, particularly if that hook happens to be the impossible one of achieving perfection! Linus, the "Peanuts" character noted, "there is no heavier burden than a great potential." Such potential combined with striving for perfection can have a paralyzing effect.

In addition to their sensitivity, these children usually have active imaginations. In relating to others they realize implications of subtle, covertly rejecting statements and attitudes, and may begin worrying whether they are accepted or loved. They may read excess meaning into ordinary situations, and even jump to conclusions. It is important to help them develop ways of checking their thoughts and fears, and to interpret meaning as it was intended by others.

Wanting to please and wanting to belong, particularly during adolescence, sometimes leads gifted children to camouflage their giftedness and to submerge themselves within "the system." Being accepted by peers at this period is important whether gifted or not, and some of these children will even intentionally fail in their schoolwork. Others merely underachieve.

The gifted child who is having difficulties relating to chronological peers may resort to withdrawal, hoping that others will come to her. It is not as uncomfortable to be without friends on purpose as it is to try to make friends only to be rebuffed. These children and their families should understand that while solitude may be a refuge of genius, all human beings need relationships with others. Solitude, though necessary, can become a prison instead of a retreat, particularly if it is sought because the child lacks social skills or feels alienated from most of the people around him.

Paradoxically, it may be the strong pressure from parents, school and society to join group activities or to make more friends that pushes some children to become "loners." Gifted children early sense their need to get away from groups if they are to pursue their unique interests at the level they consider essential. Creative people in particular require solitude to nourish their creative energies. These children may rebel if they feel that people are forcing other children on them at the expense of their own interests, even though they may want friends as well. Parents need, again, to perform a balancing act. They need to help their children find meaningful relationships with other children and adults, while protecting their right to the solitude they require. As always, priorities must be established so that neither group activities nor independent interests are supported thoughtlessly. Some creative parental guidance may help. One mother of a three year old put a large sign, "MAN THINKING," on a string around her gifted child's neck when he wished to have undisturbed time.

Questioning Traditions and Conformity Can Be a Problem

Even by early grades, gifted children may be dissatisfied with the world around them, and begin to actively question rules, customs and traditions. Their questioning and tradition-breaking often cause discomfort for family members, teachers and others who find this embarrassing, uncomfortable or challenging to their own set ways of life.

The gifted child usually values logic and rational approaches. But many traditions, customs, rules and limits are illogical, irrational or at least arbitrary, and so, they are difficult for him to accept. The result may be that the child breaks traditions or questions values and must then cope with the reactions of others. She may be called rebellious or a "Philadelphia lawyer" always looking for loopholes. Even her peers may find her tradition-breaking uncomfortable, threatening or weird — very much in conflict with the prevailing values and views.

As they grow, gifted children often have difficulty tolerating many ordinary aspects of our society. They look for consistency, and are irritated when they find inconsistencies, loopholes, and exceptions. They see facades which are socially expedient but hypocritical. Even as preschoolers, they see through grown-up foibles and games. They feel frustrated as they attempt to understand why older persons act so childishly, and why grown-ups allow obvious problems to go unsolved. Yet it appears these older persons wield so much power! How can this be? Cynicism, covering stymied idealism, often results.

Feeling frustrated and different, gifted children often become rebellious in one way or another. In younger gifted children the rebellion is usually passive, a kind of sitdown strike. Gifted teenagers, however, are more likely to rebel openly in school, at home or in society, even becoming overtly delinquent. Rebellion, whether passive or active, reflects underlying feelings of alienation. Feeling terribly out-of-step with the rest of the world, gifted teenagers may drop out of school, renounce their families, or traditional society.

By age five, six or seven many gifted children begin to worry about moral, social, humanistic, and religious concerns. Adults close by are usually puzzled by this. Could such a young child really worry about world peace or the unfairness of society? Often adults pass off the child's concerns as trivial or merely a stage. It is revealing to note that interest and worry about issues such as world peace is more common among gifted elementary children than it is among many adults.

As already stated, the most serious problem in the child's early concern for moral issues is that her ability to understand the issues intellectually far outstrips her ability to cope with the issues emotionally. She may attempt to assume adult responsibility without the emotional maturity necessary to handle human fallibility or to accept that solutions may not be readily available. In addition, adults may have told her that because of her gifts, she will be expected to assume particular responsibility for world issues when she grows up. These children are often told that they are the world's hope for the future — a heavy burden for children whose judgment, emotional maturity and tolerance for gradual change or long-term solutions may all lag far behind their intellectual capabilities.

Being Afflicted with Giftedness

Not long ago a mother opened her conversation with us by saying, "My son is afflicted with giftedness." Perhaps by this point you can understand why parents, siblings, and others may begin to wish that a child were not so "afflicted" . . . particularly if the child is *exceptionally* gifted and intensely emotionally sensitive. Adults may treat him like a computer rather than a person. The less gifted siblings may resent the focus and attention others place on the gifted one. Whenever one child in a family is identified as being gifted, other siblings in the family often react as though giftedness is an either/or thing. They think that if Johnny is gifted, then they must be "non-gifted." Jealousy, resentment, and attempts to take him down a peg follow, frequently with near disastrous results.

Thus the gifted child often receives a double message from her family and her teachers. It is obvious that her mental abilities make her different. On the one hand, family and teachers seem to appreciate, value and reward this difference. On the other hand, these same people sometimes deride the difference, may try to make the child conform to a more normal mold, or may remind her that she is not "better" than anyone else, and should not be proud of her difference.

It is this complex life situation that has prompted some persons (e.g., Hollingworth, 1975) to suggest that there is an "optimum intelligence." A person with an IQ score between 125 and 145 is bright enough so that tasks are mastered easily, but not so bright that he is noticeably different from society's mainstream, and he can feel a sense of belonging with others around him. The "optimum intelligence" range is where most leaders of our culture are likely to come from. According to this concept, those above this range are often too far removed to be accepted by most people.

Suffering Fools Gladly

The gifted child frequently begins to feel different, alienated, and alone in a world of different views and values. This is a special problem for those children with IQ scores above 160. Much of the surrounding world may seem irrational, and many people with whom they must deal, even those in positions of authority, think slowly by comparison and appear to act foolishly. The school principal, the teachers, the politician, the scoutmaster, the religious leader . . . all may say and do foolish things on many occasions. Meanwhile the gifted child finds that he can see a reasonable solution to a problem much more quickly than they. It can be frightening for the child to realize the world seems to be in the hands of these sometimes incompetent adults.

If we try to develop an appreciation for how the world looks from a gifted child's point of view, we may be able to see how even very young children may face a kind of existential crisis. The child may seriously question her own worth, or the worth of others who are less gifted. She may be plagued by feelings of sadness, anger, depression and anxiety. She may wonder whether life is worth living in a world in which she so clearly does not fit. Her world seems full of banalities, platitudes, cliches and simple-minded thinking, and apparently obvious solutions are never tried, or may be blocked by short-sighted people concerned with their immediate self-interest. If she feels that because of her gifts she must assume the lion's share of the burden of improving the lot of mankind, the odds may seem overwhelming.

Waiting For Others to Catch Up

A major task for gifted children is learning to wait for others to catch up. Recently, a gifted adult described how for so much of her life she felt like a "lady-in-waiting." In grade school she waited while others figured out solutions that were obvious to her — but she believed that in junior high it would be different. In junior high she spent as much time waiting as before — but things would be better in high school. In high school she found herself even waiting for teachers to catch up. But surely in the adult world things would be different! So she dropped out of school, and married an older, successful professional man. Now, within a fairly narrow circle of friends, she finally does not have to wait so much. But because she is female, she is cautious about showing her ideas for fear she might not be fully accepted.

Gifted children soon recognize that much of their life is spent waiting, and that their time often is "wasted" by others. Somehow these children must learn to wait, and to "suffer fools gladly," a task that they will have to continue throughout their lives (Hollingworth, 1975). Imagine living in a world where the average IQ was 50 or 60, where most others are actually retarded. Imagine that there is no other world to live in, and much of the world's productions are, in fact, mediocre. The challenge, then, is whether we could learn to live gladly in that world, with personal contentment, sharing and joy, or whether we would be angry, depressed, withdrawn and miserable . . . perhaps finally deciding that such a life was not worth living.

The key to contentment is primarily a matter of attitude — the way one views the world. If a gifted child is given loving guidance, he can usually turn waiting time into opportunities. He can creatively fill this time through engaging in detailed observations, maintaining a steady supply of books or other extra stimulation of his own choice, or perhaps sharing his understanding and knowledge with another person who is trying to catch-up. Through nurturing and guidance, the gifted child can come to see that humans who are not as bright or as quick nevertheless do have value. Traits other than intelligence, such as love, valor, loyalty, generosity, willingness to work, and desire for a better world, are important also.

The Antidote:
Emotions Within a Solid Self-Concept

How can you help a child learn tolerance and acceptance? Clearly mental "giftedness" is valuable; but living comfortably with yourself and others is even more important. It does a person no good to be incredibly bright if at the same time she is also incredibly miserable or has such emotional impairment that she functions destructively. History has demonstrated many cases of persons who were highly gifted intellectually, but whose self-concept and emotions were so disturbed that entire countries, and even the world, have suffered as a result of their misguided intelligence.

A major key is in helping gifted children develop understanding of themselves, a positive self-concept, and specific stress-management procedures. The gifted child's strengths in quick comprehension of concepts and good verbal and conceptual ability allow rapid acquisition of stress-reduction approaches.

Although gifted children and their families are somewhat more likely to encounter certain kinds of stress, this does *not* mean that all gifted persons will have emotional problems or will be maladjusted! If parents, teachers and others are aware of the common stresses, and appreciate that these children can learn stress-reduction techniques much earlier than most persons realize, then the children can be taught early to overcome potentially destructive stress situations.

Feelings Are Important

By now it should be apparent that a major emphasis must be placed on helping the gifted child recognize his feelings, label them accordingly, and use them as tools for growth. Until he recognizes his feelings as acceptable and important, it is extremely difficult, perhaps impossible, for him to develop a good concept of himself as a competent person, beyond just being gifted which is, after all, a condition he did not create for himself. Gifted children need to be assured that it is okay to explore their feelings, and that feelings have no "right" or "wrong." The way he expresses those feelings in action may be right or wrong, but the feelings themselves are automatic, reflexive, and simply part of human nature. The behavioral expression of these feelings can, and should, be acceptably shaped over time. Limits are, indeed, very important! It is shaping that we generally call socialization.

Talking about feelings with gifted children requires special sensitivity. Because they may be uncomfortable discussing feelings, they tend to lead the conversation onto more comfortable ground, asking questions about facts, endeavoring to concentrate on what they know or can learn empirically and avoiding opinions and emotions, which seem more risky. But they need to appreciate early in life that emotions are powerful and that feelings are frequently illogical. Gifted children, like other people who would be well-adjusted, must learn to be aware of their feelings and to express and communicate them appropriately.

The gifted child who has not learned to interpret her feelings, particularly after enduring numerous discouraging statements, rejections and criticisms, usually loses her motivation. This is even more likely when she is not allowed to voice her opinions or complaints at home or at school, when there is no caring person to whom she can communicate her reactions and concerns. We are convinced that discouragement of gifted children accounts for findings (Marland, 1972) which report that the majority of gifted children work at least two to four grade levels below their potential.

Lighting the Fire

Parents and teachers can take specific steps to help a gifted child become positively motivated, to encourage desirable behaviors, and to help the child develop a good self-concept. In the case of a self-defeating and apparently unmotivated gifted child, the parents and teachers need to remember that they must start where the child is, no matter how negatively motivated he seems at the time. It usually does no good to demand that the child initially meet your high goals. If the child is turned off, chances are he is not interested in doing something just because *you* want to do it. The initial goal must be small and easily attainable. Presumably you are more flexible right now than he!

Once you decide to begin by trying to understand why apparently unmotivated behavior seems to be preferred by the child, there are many useful techniques and skills you can use. Many of these specific steps are discussed later in the chapter on motivation. It is important to realize that a gifted child who is turned off may require quite a while before showing glimmers of motivation (at least in those areas teachers and parents would like!). Although progress may be slow, and the degree of improvement may be small, patience must be great. Motivate yourself by remembering that this child may transfer motivation from one area to another! Often gifted children are highly motivated for those things *they* wish to do, although they may not desire things that *others* want them to do. With patience and care their motivation can usually be redirected and transferred to more desirable areas, particularly as the child's self-concept improves. For example, a gifted child may care little for penmanship and spelling until she is encouraged to prepare a collection for public display, or to send a poem to a magazine for publication, or to write a letter to one of her heroes.

Self-Motivation, Self-Discipline and Self-Concept

It is important to help the child recognize who is pulling his strings, then, ultimately, the goal is to help him to pull his own strings, to set his own goals — and to believe in himself.

Helping the gifted child feel good about himself also means helping him feel good about his place in the world. Beyond becoming just tolerant of others, it is important to help him develop empathy for those who are less gifted. If a gifted child can learn to appreciate how the world looks through others' eyes and can put himself in the shoes of others, he will have fewer frustrations. This includes thinking through problems and situations as they appear to others, rather than just writing others off as "morons." The gifted child must learn self-discipline, patience and understanding. Role-playing and activities that require interdependency seem to be particularly effective with gifted children, and can be used at a very early age to help them appreciate the attitudes, feelings and worth that others have in various situations.

In summary, more important than being gifted is feeling good about oneself, feeling that what one does is important, and that one fits with the world. A goal for gifted children is to help them realize that though they are different, they have much in common with others. Gifted children have the same basic human feelings and needs for belonging and self-respect as other children, although the gifted child may feel these needs more keenly and may want emotional satisfaction more intensely than other children. Certainly they are *children* and cannot be expected to "find their own way." They need special guidance and help.

A central task, both for us and our gifted children, revolves around the issues of *differences*. We seem terribly ambivalent about differences — maybe because our society is so conformist. Perhaps the human animal, being social, *must* be conformist. Our cultural heritage leads us to believe that the individual is important, even paramount. But the practical needs of a working society are necessarily based on identifying groups and treating their members as interchangeable units. Thus, there seems to be a fundamental cultural ambivalence regarding individual differences.

As parents of gifted children, you deal daily with differences, as clearly as do parents of handicapped children. The mother who reads Gesell (Ilg & Ames, 1955) may find that her two and a half year old is already doing what is listed under five or six year olds in Gesell. She quickly knows that she is raising a child who does not fit the norm. What does she do with this information? Those who seek out support from the "experts" repeatedly hear the statement "the child is a child first, and is only gifted secondarily." But we cannot separate gifted children into bits, as if they were really normal children who fit the usual mold but with some extras tacked on like lace adornments.

Gifted children are not simply decorated normal children — they are, indeed, fundamentally different. A child with IQ 145 is as different from the normal IQ of 100 as is the child of IQ 55. Few professionals would advise parents of a 55 IQ child to treat her *first* as a child, and only incidentally as retarded. For children above 145 IQ, their intellectual potential — the brain that drives them — is so fundamental to *everything* about them, that it cannot be separated from the personhood of the child. The higher the IQ, the more so. We must begin with a recognition that these children *are* different, but then help them learn social, interpersonal and self-development skills to relate to the rest of humanity.

A balance must be struck between "identity" and "comparison with others." A parent must learn to accept the child's identity as it exists *in itself,* rather than as compared with some norm which applies to most others. Unless a parent sees that identity and truly finds it acceptable, it is hard for the parent to encourage the child to accept himself.

We also realize that we have to deal in comparisons because we live in a world of other people; but the comparisons should not be the primary focus of our interactions with our child. We are constantly walking a tightrope — trying to avoid over-stressing differences, while having to admit them in order to cope. One gifted child described it in *On Being Gifted* (1978) as follows:

> "'Gifted and talented' is not something you can
> take up lightly on free weekends. It's something
> that's going to affect everything about your life,
> twenty-four hours a day, 365-1/4 days a year. It's

something that can force you into being mature before you might be ready; it's something
that can go all wrong on you and leave you
torn apart."

It is essential to incorporate the basics of humanness in the
guidance of gifted children, even if it must be at the expense
of their learning a few more facts! Gifted children must come
to know that there are people who understand and care, and
who realize that being gifted sometimes hurts. They must come
to know that others share their ways of viewing the world, and
they must develop a sense of value for many ordinary things
and ordinary people. One person who understood the dilemma
was George Bernard Shaw who, tongue-in cheek, stated:

"The reasonable man adapts himself to the
world around him. The unreasonable man ex-
pects the world to adapt itself to him. Therefore
all progress is made by unreasonable men."

But the gifted child must learn to be a reasonable person — at
least some of the time — and must develop an awareness that
lets him know when he is being unreasonable. He needs help in
learning that "unreasonable" can have two meanings — being
genuinely irrational on the one hand, or just being different in
the eyes of the rest of society. The gifted child needs help in
sorting out which way he is being unreasonable. He must learn
when to stick by his stand in spite of the perceptions of
others, and when it is more prudent to drop it. He may have
to learn to compromise, but needs the strength of character to
refuse compromise sometimes as well. He must learn to be
comfortable with himself during those times. A strong self-
concept is vital for gifted children, and their emotional development deserves more attention than it has received by parents,
teachers and other professionals.

References

American Association of Gifted Children. *On Being Gifted*. New York: Walker and Co., 1978.

Coleman, D. 1528 Little geniuses and how they grew. *Psychology Today*, 1980, 13 (9) Feb., 28-43.

Cronbach, L.J. Essentials of Psychology Testing. (2nd Ed.) N.Y.: Harper, 1960.

Fox, L.H. Identification of the academically gifted. *American Psychologist*, 1981, 36 (10, 1103-1111.

Garfield, E. Will a bright mind make its own way? *Current Contents*, 1980, No. 51, 5-15.

Hollingworth, L.S. *Children Above 180 IQ*. New York: Arno Press, 1975 (Reprint of 1942 edition)

Ilg, F.L. and Ames, L.B. *The Gesell Institute's Child Behavior from Birth to Ten*. N.Y.: Harper and Row, 1955.

Kane, N. and Kane, M. Comparison of right and left hemisphere functions. *The Gifted Child Quarterly*, 1979, 23 (1), Spring, 157-167.

Lemov, P. That kid is smart. *The Washingtonian*, 1979, 15 (3)., 225-233.

Lipper, A. Gifted and Talented Children. *The Congressional Record*, Vol. 125, Wed., September 5, 1979.

Lyons, H.C. Our most neglected natural resource. *Today's Education*, 1981, Feb.-March, 15-19.

Marland, S. *Education of the Gifted and Talented*, U.S. Commission of Education, 92nd Cong., 2nd Session, Washington, D.C.: USCPO, 1972.

Tannenbaum, A.J. and Neuman, E. *Somewhere to Turn: Strategies for Parents of Gifted and Talented Children*. New York: Teachers College Press, Columbia Univ., 1980.

Terman, L.M. *Genetic Studies of Genius. Vol. I. Mental and Physical Traits of a Thousand Gifted Children*. Stanford: Stanford Univ. Press, 1925.

Williams, A. Teaching gifted students how to deal with stress. *The Gifted Child Quarterly*, 1979, Spring, 23 (1), 136-141.

"To improve the golden moment of opportunity,
and catch the good that is within our reach, is
the great art of life."

Samuel Johnson

"Do not wait for extraordinary circumstances to
do good; try to use ordinary situations."

Jean Paul Richter

CHAPTER II

SOME PROBLEMS, PERHAPS . . . BUT MANY MORE OPPORTUNITIES!

Support and positive reinforcement from parents, teachers and other adults play a major role in determining the gifted child's self-concept and in his educational and creative development. We teach what we are, and some adults provide outstanding models that guide gifted children to successfully pattern their lives emotionally and occupationally. What characterizes these people that makes them so effective with gifted children?

Paul Torrance (1981), a noted author on the topic of creativity, studied several groups of gifted and creative children for many years. Years later he asked them to reflect on "teachers who made a difference" in their lives. Recurring distinguishing characteristics were apparent. These common traits are summarized in Table 3.

Although Torrance focused on teachers, we believe these same behaviors and approaches apply to "parents who make a difference," or to any adult. Encouragement, acceptance as a person, sharing of interest and excitement — these are critical to the healthy development of a person's sense of self-worth and to his obtaining a life-long desire for learning and creating. These same characteristics were also noted by gifted students in their book, *On Being Gifted* (American Association for Gifted Children, 1978).

Table 3

About people
who made a difference to gifted children:

- "She encouraged active participation with others, asked lots of questions, and accepted all answers without humiliating me; she helped me feel competent, even while I was trying something new."
- "She conveyed a powerful feeling of my ability to comprehend and to do things, and it seemed that I was able to share this excitement with her. She understood it, welcomed and enjoyed it herself which left me with a sense that learning is exciting and something that's good to share."
- "He encouraged us to fall in love with something and some of us are still pursuing it as the center of our future career image."
- "He gave individual encouragement and focused privately on my own needs; he conveyed that it's important to him that I suceed and that I like myself."

All of these special people:
- Communicated that the child, his beliefs, his feelings, and his behaviors were important.
- Facilitated identification, expression and acceptance of the child's feelings.
- Conveyed understanding and acceptance of their own feelings.
- Made it clear that they cherished the whole child — not just his abilities or achievements.
- Expressed that they valued his unique qualities.
- Allowed or encouraged him to pursue his special interests.
- Set aside some focused time to share with the child.
- Gave encouragement and support for attempts, not just for successes.
- Emphasized the value of productive cooperation and were, themselves, models that sharing worked.

Such support is particularly important for the gifted child who feels out of step with the world around her. She especially needs home to be a haven where she can recharge her batteries, and where people in that home can help her understand, untangle, and accept (not necessarily agree with) the existence of the many strange behaviors of our world outside.

Where home is that kind of haven, and where one or two teachers, neighbors or other adults make a difference by emotionally supporting the gifted child's self-concept, these children will thrive. They are able to actualize their mental potential in creative ways that benefit themselves and society. Supplying support and encouragement at home not only provides good models of attractive behavior, but also inoculates the child against interpersonal pressures that he will encounter in the future.

This concept of inoculation has been used quite beneficially in medicine, but can be applied to emotions as well. It seems, for example, that positive experiences with one exceptionally supportive adult enable a child to withstand negative experiences from several other adults. One professional called it an "inoculation ratio" of one to six, and pointed out that in school one terrific teacher allows a child to survive at least four mediocre and two very poor teachers! This same sort of inoculation ratio appears to hold with regard to human relations outside the classroom. The positive self-regard acquired from one person allows him to mentally discount the stresses of destructive criticism, blame or even ridicule that he may encounter elsewhere.

Parent Groups: An Attempt to Inoculate

The best way to solve problems is to prevent them or to build defenses and problem-solving techniques for those likely to arise. If problems exist, we can use them as opportunities for inoculation and growth. We are aware that gifted children and their families may be at higher risk for encountering certain kinds of stresses or psychological problems. We also recognize that intellectually gifted children have a potential to achieve satisfying emotional adjustment.

Encountering stresses does not *necessarily* lead to emotional problems. It can, instead, lead to greater emotional strength and greater tolerance for ambiguity and complexity. Stress tolerance and stress management contribute to the perserverance that permits people to create and enjoy. When gifted children are helped to learn techniques for handling stress, are taught coping skills, and are provided with emotional and intellectual enrichment, they can be exciting, creative, and in harmony with themselves and others.

Our belief is that the most effective means for supportive guidance and problem prevention must lie with the parents. While educational enrichment or other special programs are for a limited time, a parent of a gifted child will be around much longer. Studies continue to confirm that the most significant influence on a child's personality and performance is the behavior of his parents. Emotional enrichment and development begin in infancy and the preschool years, and major dimensions of personality are set by the time the child reaches school age. Unfortunately, most formal programs for gifted children outside the family do not focus on special needs of these children until age eight or older, so in the early years it is the parents who must provide virtually all the support.

In response to the need for greater understanding and encouragement of gifted children within their families, the authors have developed a program for parents. Though the emphasis is focused on younger children, the groups contain parents of children of all ages. The parents meet in group sessions with the group co-leaders (one of whom is a psychologist) to discuss particular topics that relate to emotional and interpersonal concerns. Parents report that they have found unique help and support within these groups. We hope that similar groups can be formed in other communities for similar purposes.

The content of these guidance groups is practical, with little emphasis on theory. It is the specific practical attitude and behavior change techniques that are most helpful to parents. They have heard enough glittering generalities and goals — what they want to know is how to achieve these goals!

The guidance discussion groups are conducted as a series. One major topic is the focus for each session, and the series consists of the following ten topics:

Identification: Tests and Characteristics
Motivation
Discipline
Stress Management
Communication of Feelings
Peer Relationships
Sibling Relationships
Tradition-Breaking
Depression
Parent Relationships

These topics were chosen because they are frequent problem areas encountered specifically by gifted children, their siblings and their parents. In each session the parents share situations and common experiences and concerns. The group leaders and other parents offer comment, advice and guidance.

It is important to note that the groups are *not* therapy groups, nor are they Encounter groups, Sensitivity groups, T-groups, etc. Rather they are guidance groups concerned with handling life situations that could possibly get out of hand. As a colleague recently remarked, "there are two kinds of people in this world — those who have problems, and others you don't know well enough yet to know what their problems are." We are aware that life has problems, and we discuss preventive behaviors that can be employed, along with methods for encouraging positive growth. Often it is possible to make a potential problem work for you in a healthy, growth-oriented fashion, rather than to passively accept its negative consequences.

If the situations are already causing serious problems, parents are referred to other professionals for individual help, usually in addition to attending the group sessions. Several psychologists have affiliated themselves with us as resource persons. We recognize that we are fortunate in this regard. Many parents have told us that they have had great difficulty finding a mental health professional who understands the problems of gifted children and their families.

From the information we are providing, it is possible for others to start groups similar to ours. We hope to provide consultation and training to interested persons.[2] One particular caution has become apparent; it is important that a suitably qualified mental health professional guide the group. Professional monitoring, control, and occasional intervention is required to prevent some meetings from turning into group therapy or gripe sessions. Sometimes emotions are so strong that parents will blurt out their overwhelming life situations with such personal pain and detail that some group members become intensely uncomfortable. At other times, the personal traits of a group member may be such an obvious problem that the remaining group members begin to confront, blame, or even verbally attack that person. In our experience, training and skilled professional monitoring are essential to guide progressive

---

[2] Additional information about program consultation can be obtained through writing the authors at the School of Professional Psychology, Wright State University, Dayton, Ohio 45435

discussion, to highlight key points, and to remind group members that insights and behavior changes cannot be bludgeoned into others.

Do Not Try to
Accomplish Everything In One Week

The parent group sessions are held one or two weeks apart. Experience suggests that at least a week is needed between topics to allow participants to absorb the various aspects of each topic as it relates to their own families. This period also allows time for them to try some of the specific suggestions.

In reading this material as written you may wish to follow a similar pattern — that is, read one topic and give yourself time to reflect on and implement it. An alternative approach, which may be more effective, is to read the entire text of the book, and then return to each topic section for more study. In either approach, the point is "Do not try to take on all the topics at once!" Start with one area, accomplish it, and then build on it.

About the Ten Topics

For each of the ten topics we have prepared a chapter that gives basic information about that subject. These discussions provide a framework that we hope will lead you to a better understanding of each area as well as a re-evaluation of many misconceptions. The contents of these chapters contain much of the materials used in our parents' groups, and build on the information contained in Chapter I. Sometimes, for emphasis, we have restated earlier ideas. At the end of each of the next ten chapters we have included a brief question and answer series to elaborate on some questions that we are often asked.

Many of the points raised within each topic are simply basic to good parenting — they do not apply only to gifted children. We have included them to provide a framework within which you can consider those points that do relate specifically to guiding gifted children.

Basic good parenting is necessary whether a child is gifted or not. It is not enough just to love a child — you also must know what you're doing! Gifted children, like all other children, need limits, discipline and guidance. They also need to be encouraged, nurtured, stimulated and challenged in their encounters with the world, as well as the freedom to experience the natural consequences of their behaviors. Only in this way can they learn to set priorities and to structure their own lives. Through the responsible caring and guidance of adults, these children develop personal integrity, a workable system of values and ethics, and social responsibility. At the same time they can develop an appreciation for the value of recreation, leisure and stress management. As with all children, the goal is that they come to know, trust and value themselves, and to feel they belong.

We hope that you find these chapters helpful. We would appreciate comments from our readers concerning them.

References

American Association of Gifted Children. *On Being Gifted.* New York: Walker and Co., 1978.

Torrance, P. Predicting the Creativity of Elementary School Children and the Teachers Who Made a Difference. *Gifted Child Quarterly,* 1981, Vol. XXV, 56-62.

44

"If something exists, it exists in some amount. If it exists in some amount, it can be measured."

Edward L. Thorndike

"Intelligence is the global capacity of an individual to act purposefully, to think rationally and to deal effectively with his environment."

David Wechsler

"The IQ obtained on a standard individual intelligence test has more demonstrated behavioral correlates than any other psychological measure. . . . The intelligence test gives a better estimate of potential than other measures of achievement."

Jerome Sattler

"We must guard against defining intelligence solely in terms of ability to pass the tests of a given intelligence scale. It should go without saying that no existing scale is capable of adequately measuring the ability to deal with all possible kinds of material on all intelligence levels."

Lewis Terman

"The test of a first-rate intelligence is the ability to hold two opposed ideas at the same time, and still retain the ability to function."

F. Scott Fitzgerald

CHAPTER III

IDENTIFYING AND TESTING THE GIFTED

Intelligence has always been a matter of much discussion, and clearly is not a simple concept. Attempts to generate a precise, agreed upon definition have been elusive, and even now agreement exists only in general. Nevertheless, there *is* widespread recognition that high intelligence exists, and that intelligence may be expressed in many different ways — not just one way.

As noted in Chapter I, significant differences occur among gifted children. They probably are a more intellectually diverse group than average children. Yet, gifted children do have intellectual characteristics in common. These shared traits have been described in detail in several other publications (e.g., Clark, 1979) and are summarized in Table 4.

How much of each of these characteristics is needed in order to call a child gifted? Compared to what? Does a child have to excel in all of these areas or behaviors? Who decides when a child meets enough of these criteria to qualify and on what basis?

Experts continue to debate the best definition of giftedness, and to discuss definitions of other terms such as "genius," "talent," "intelligence." These debates are worthwhile and will lead to better understanding of our children, but parents, school systems and others cannot wait for these issues to be settled.

Table 4

Typical Intellectual Characteristics of Gifted Children
— Unusually large vocabularies for their age — Ability to read earlier than most children, often before entering school — Greater comprehension of the subtleties of language — Longer attention span, persistence and intense concentration — Ability to learn basic skills more quickly and with less practice — Wide range of interests — Highly developed curiosity and a limitless supply of questions — Interest in experimenting and doing things differently — Tendency to put ideas or things together in ways that are unusual and not obvious (divergent thinking) — Ability to retain a great deal of information — Unusual sense of humor

In practical terms, much actual identification of gifted children is currently done by teachers — based either on their observations of classroom behavior, or on group achievement tests. It is these teacher-identified children who constitute most gifted programs. Identifying gifted children on the basis of teacher nomination, however, overlooks many gifted children. Several studies (e.g., Jacobs, 1971) have shown that teacher nomination correctly identifies less than half of students later found to be gifted through individual testing. Usually, the errors overlook gifted students, although about 10% of the students identified by teachers as intellectually gifted actually were not. Even exceptionally gifted students are not immune from oversight. As many as 25% are missed by teachers, (Marland Report, 1972).

Group tests are another common approach to identifying gifted students. Although these usually are tests of achievement, they are used by school systems as though they were tests of intelligence. School personnel typically assume that children who achieve in the 90th percentile or above, are the ones gifted intellectually. Such an assumption is not always true, however, for several reasons. First, children in the earlier grades sometimes score high on achievement tests out of extremely high motivation. Sometimes this intense determination is called over-achievement. Their intellectual ability may, in fact, only be somewhat above average. Second, many gifted children are not motivated to demonstrate their abilities in the standardized format of achievement tests. They may even be hindered because of their creative approaches or because these tests rely too heavily on verbal, rather than other, skills. Gifted children with learning disabilities or developmental lags typically show a highly variable pattern on the subparts of these tests, though their total scores may appear average. Finally, these achievement tests ordinarily contain a limited number of items so that missing or skipping only one or two items can result in a drop of five or ten percentile points.

Group tests of intelligence have the same limitations as group achievement tests; thus these group tests also do not identify almost half the gifted children tested. Further, it appears that the most highly gifted children are penalized the most by group test scores. The discrepancy between group test scores and individual intelligence test scores increases as the child's level of intelligence approaches to the upper extreme.

Thus, parents should not be too quick to give up the notion that their child may be gifted if their own observations seem convincing to them. Where possible, they should talk with the teachers to share observations and information, or talk with the child's nurse or pediatrician. Even where there is some doubt whether the child is "just above average" or whether he is gifted, we recommend that the parents act *as if* the child is gifted — at least until the second or third grade in school. By this, we are not recommending great pressure, but we are recommending support, enrichment and encouragement to develop his self-worth and confidence.

To get the most realistic appraisal of potential, parents may decide to have individual intellectual and achievement evaluation of their child by a qualified psychologist or school psychologist. They may arrange testing simply to get more information for appropriate planning purposes, or to get a baseline of the child's current functioning in order to negotiate an alternative course of action in the child's school. Parents of gifted children need to become informed about psychological tests and the testing procedures as well as about characteristics of gifted children. Even if parents do not seek testing, they need to become knowledgeable since schools usually use tests for placement. Even though these placement decisions are determined significantly by various psychological and educational tests, school administrators often have little clinical training. Their training in statistics, tests and measurements may be less than that of many parents.

Testing takes the evaluation about someone largely out of the realm of subjective impression. Compared with group testing, individual testing has some particular benefits. When done on an individual basis, testing gives more opportunity to insure that distractions do not reduce the child's performance and that the child is focusing his best attention and effort during testing. Because it is standardized, testing gives a bench-mark that allows a child's mental functioning to be compared with that of others her own age. Such testing can be important, particularly when objective data are needed to convince school personnel that a particular action may be needed. Some parents have told us, however, of school officials who insist that even high scores on individually administered tests "must be inaccurate." Then a psychologist may need to become an ally to explain to school authorities supportive data about the tests used.

The Renzulli Model

Identification of gifted children within school systems usually involves three elements that overlap as shown in Figure 3. In this widely used model, developed by Renzulli and Smith (1980), a child is identified to participate in a gifted program only when these three elements overlap substantially. Another way of stating the Renzulli model is that superior ability, itself, is not enough — there must also be high motivation to use that ability, and it must be expressed in creative ways, or to an unusual degree. Because it insists on the clear *expression* of giftedness, use of the Renzulli model overlooks many gifted children who, for a variety of reasons, are unable or unwilling to demonstrate their talents in the ways being measured. For example, gifted children with cerebral palsy, learning disabilities or hearing and vision impairments are often not identified as gifted.

Figure 3

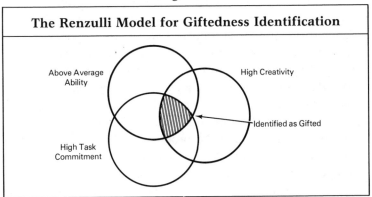

The Renzulli Model for Giftedness Identification

Above Average Ability

High Creativity

High Task Commitment

Identified as Gifted

It is not unusual to find a child with high intelligence and high IQ scores who shows low school achievement in mediocre or low grades, or even low scores on standardized achievement tests. These children need extra encouragement or even professional help. As will be discussed in later chapters, we believe something is discouraging or preventing them from expressing their ability. This could be a motivational problem, a learning block or disability, or an emotional problem such as depression or anxiety. Possibly it could be a clash between the child's learning style and the school's teaching style. In the case of children in the highest ranges, it could also be the inappropriateness of typical school materials.

Since the Renzulli model is so widely accepted, and since it emphasizes demonstrated achievement of classroom material, it is important to note that not all children learn in the same fashion or have the same "kind" of intelligence. In addition to individual differences, there seem to be strong sex differences. Up through elementary school ages, girls generally learn better if materials are presented verbally; boys, if materials are presented graphically or visually. Most of the material in these school settings, however, stresses verbal skills and approaches. It may interest some parents to note that sex differences reverse as adulthood is reached — most men learn better verbally.

The verbal emphasis in schools, particularly the early grades, often is a handicap for minority children. Many of these children were raised in families and neighborhoods where the language used differs from that traditionally used in schools, and where broad access to verbal concepts and complex stimulation has been limited. Identification of minority gifted children is, then, much more difficult, and the problems stemming from group tests and teacher nomination are magnified.

Some children, particularly gifted ones, think and learn best in still other ways that may be quite unusual. Some of these gifted children think musically, or situationally, or through visualizing mentally via mathematical or spatial relations. Others learn best when they physically are doing a task, such as the gifted child who learned the elements of the chemical table by dancing them, first physically and then by imagining herself dancing.

Right Brain/Left Brain

Some exciting new notions about intelligence and achievement have recently surfaced in discussions of "right brain" and "left brain" children. Although obviously everyone uses both brain hemispheres, research has suggested that some people predominantly use one brain hemisphere more than the other. This brain side dominance is related to distinct differences in a person's style of thinking, problem solving, achievement and intelligence. Some of these differences are summarized in Table 5.

Persons who are "left-brained" are more concerned with the processes of logic, analysis, facts, details and organization, and prefer verbal approaches to problems. Persons with specialized right brain dominance prefer visual explanations, use images, and synthesize in fluid, abstract, intuitive ways.

Which way is better? It depends on what task is at hand. In our society there clearly are places for both. The right-brained person makes a much better artist or musician or perhaps theoretical physicist. The left-brained person would be superior as a chemist or accountant.

But what if you are a right-brained child in a classroom being taught by a left-brained teacher? It may be like trying to mix oil and water, or trying to teach a dolphin to type. The teacher wants organized, logical, verbal techniques of learning; the child learns best, and prefers, intuitive, visual, open methods.

For parents of right-brained children, it may help to remember that *most* school tasks and expectations emphasize left-brain processes.

Table 5

Some Preferred Ways of Knowing According to Hemispheric Specialization[3]	
Left brain specialization:	Right brain specialization:
— Prefers verbal explanations	— Prefers visual explanations
— Uses language to remember	— Uses images to remember
— Processes information sequentially	— Process information holistically
— Produces ideas logically	— Produces ideas intuitively
— Prefers concrete thinking tasks	— Prefers abstract thinking tasks
— Deals with one task at a time	— Deals with several tasks at a time
— Prefers analyzing activities	— Prefers synthesizing activities
— Prefers proper working materials	— Improvises with materials available
— Likes structured experiences	— Likes open, fluid experiences
— Prefers to learn facts and details	— Prefers to gain general overview
— Approaches problems seriously	— Approaches problems playfully

[3] Adapted from E. Paul Torrance, Your Style of Learning and Thinking, *The Gifted Child Quarterly*, 1977, Vol. XXI, No. 4, Winter.

General measures of achievement or intelligence through group tests typically rely heavily on left-brain functions. Because of this they do not provide sufficient information about patterns of specific abilities and levels of achievement for appropriate program placement. Particularly for right-brained children, their thinking approaches to creative problem solving are not sufficiently measured by typical group achievement, aptitude or intelligence tests.

Intelligence Tests

Tests of intelligence only measure a child's functioning and potential as it appears at the time of testing. Not all children have good days all the time. Emotional upsets, illnesses, fear of the testing situation, lack of intellectual stimulation and other factors can cause downward fluctuations in the child's intelligence test scores. The test scores are meaningful only in the context of the child's life situation, and it is for these reasons that a responsible psychologist is required to interpret them. It is essential that the psychologist have good judgment, as well as good skills in relating to people. The psychologist must help parents and others realize that an IQ score is not a sacred, unchangeable number; it is only a helpful piece of information from a standardized situation that allows some reasonably accurate predictions to be made, provided good professional judgment is used.

As we have noted earlier, intelligence is not the same as achievement, and intelligence tests are not the same as achievement tests. An intelligence test measures potential broadly and some ability areas specifically. Achievement tests measure what the child expresses he has learned so far within that narrow area. Specific talents and areas of creativity are related to intelligence and achievement, but are not the same. Special tests exist for measuring specific talents in music and other artistic areas, and for assessing various fields of creativity.

A long-standing controversy has existed concerning how much of intelligence is inherited, and how much is determined by environment. Most of the studies of this have focused on identical twins who were raised in different families from birth. The results have indicated that about 60% to 70% of the similarity in IQ scores is due to inherited ability (Sattler, 1982). It would not be correct, however, to assume that the gifted and talented come from privileged environments. Twenty to thirty percent come from parents representing skilled and unskilled labor or rural backgrounds. Gifted children include persons from all ethnic groups and lifestyles.

Environment clearly has an impact on intelligence. Intelligence can be heightened through nurturance and hindered through neglect and abuse. Children, particularly young children, often show a significant increase in intelligence as a result of increased emotional support and intellectual stimulation. IQ scores may increase by ten, twenty or more points.

Although "intelligence" is a general characteristic, it is comprised of numerous separate component elements which may vary widely in their potential level or in the amount of their development. Sometimes a child of high general intellectual ability will have one or more specific areas (such as mathematics) that are below average in development. This situation is called a "learning disability." Some gifted children are also learning disabled — a very frustrating situation!

The most often used individual (rather than group) intelligence tests for children are: the *Wechsler Intelligence Scale for Children* — Revised (WISC-R) for age six and up and the *Wechsler Pre-School and Primary Scale of Intelligence* (WPPSI) for ages four through six. They measure verbal aspects of intelligence ("Verbal IQ") separated from visual-spatial intelligence

("Performance IQ"). This corresponds to some degree with left-brain and right-brain functioning since the left hemisphere is the location involving activities mostly reflected by Verbal IQ, while the right hemisphere is more concerned with performance IQ functions such as spatial relations.

In addition to being divided into "Verbal" and "Performance" areas, each of the two general areas of the WISC-R and WPPSI is composed of six separate subtests. These measure factors such as general information, verbal abstracting ability, visual abstraction/organization, and ability to use symbols.

The *Stanford-Binet Intelligence Scale* is also frequently used for children's testing, particularly preschool children. It begins with a two year old level and goes to an adult level, and involves about six different types of tasks at each yearly level. Although the "Binet" does not have separate Verbal and Performance IQ scores, this test has the potential advantage of having a higher ceiling score particularly for children age six or younger.

Individual tests of intelligence are reasonably accurate at age five or six. The stability/accuracy increases up to about age fourteen. Beyond this age the scores generally remain quite stable. For younger children the actual IQ scores may vary from testing to testing due to the various factors noted earlier. For children age six to eight the variation in IQ score will be less than 8 points in 85 to 90% of the cases — accurate enough for most situations. It is also noteworthy that when an IQ score is inaccurate, it is probably in a conservative direction — that is, an underestimate. The tests are designed so that it is unlikely a child will obtain a high score by chance.

With gifted children, it is helpful to get intelligence and achievement testing at about age five and again at ten or eleven. This enables realistic expectations and planning within his school. Otherwise most school systems will not provide intellectual assessment unless a problem is noted, and achievement tests and teacher nominations may not identify the child as gifted until he is about age ten. According to some studies (e.g., Bloom, 1964) about 50% of a child's intellectual potential is developed by age four, and 80% by age eight. Early identification may allow parents and school systems to prevent, rather than attempt to cure, underachievement.

It is important to remember that the abilities that constitute intelligence do not develop at a constant, smooth rate. Until puberty, some children appear to have genetically based developmental trends where their intellectual growth pattern, like their physical growth pattern, is a series of spurts and pauses. When individual growth patterns vary significantly, retesting may be needed to determine the extent that developmental lags may be hindering the child's achievement or other functioning.

It is sometimes best to get the testing done outside the school system since you may intend to negotiate alternative provisions within the school. Sometimes, too, the school may be part of a problem with the child, and the parents may wish independent information. Parents also need to consider that many school psychologists have received little training in meeting the special needs of gifted students or even in broad clinical areas. They spend most of their time focusing on children with learning problems, particularly handicapping learning conditions. Similarly, however, many clinical psychologists have received little training in working with gifted children. It is appropriate to ask professionals inside or outside school systems about credentials, licenses, and areas of formal specialty training.

Second opinions and reevaluations are now acceptable practice in psychology. These options are valuable particularly if you think the psychologist or school system is not using psychological testing properly or has obtained an inaccurate assessment.

Every state has a Director of Programs for the Gifted (see Chapter XV). From this office, you can be directed to the closest coordinator of gifted educational programs who, in turn, can be a source of resources and referral. The coordinators of gifted programs we have known are enthusiastically caring and co-operative, and dedicated to bringing out the best in others. They are among our favorite people.

In summary, it is important to realize that you do not need to depend solely on your local school personnel to determine whether your child is gifted. Other resources are available, including professionals who can give individual intelligence and achievement tests. Your observations and judgment are important since even individual intelligence tests have limitations. In identification remember that many gifted children do not demonstrate their abilities through their achievement in school. The chapters which follow contain more information and discussion on underachievement, motivation and related areas.

References

Bloom, B.S. *Stability and Change in Human Characteristics.* New York: John Wiley and Sons, 1964.

Clark, B. *Growing Up Gifted.* Columbus, Ohio: Charles Merrill Co., 1979.

Jacobs, J. Effectiveness of Teacher and Parent Identification of Gifted Children as a Function of School Level. *Psychology in the Schools,* 1971, *8* 140-142.

Marland, S. *Education of the Gifted & Talented,* U.S. Commission of Education, 92nd Cong., 2nd Session, Washington, D.C.: USGPO, 1972.

Renzulli, J. and Smith, L.H. An alternative approach to identifying and programming for gifted and talented students. *G/C/T,* 1980, Nov./Dec., 4-11.

Sattler, J. *Assessment of Children's Intelligence and Special Abilities.* Boston: Allyn and Bacon, Inc., 1982.

Some Frequent Questions
About Identification of Gifted Children

Our child has been identified as gifted to us, but how about to herself? Should I tell my child she is gifted? I'm afraid she will get big-headed and feel that she is different from others.

In one way or another you will need to explain to your child that she is gifted. By the age of three or four she will begin to be aware that she *is* different from other children, and by the time she enters school she will need some explanation of this. Otherwise she will provide or even manufacture her own explanations, such as that she is unlikeable, or that other children have little value. Since many gifted children dislike the term, "gifted," you do not need to use that word. You may instead use the words such as "special" or "quick" or "talented" or "fast learner." Whatever word is used, it is important to point out repeatedly that other children have special talents that are different from hers but no less valuable. It is this repeated reminder of interdependency with others that will help prevent vanity.

What about early admission and skipping grades? What is the emotional impact of this?

Half of gifted children have taught themselves to read before school entry. Some learn to read by age two, and many by age four. In light of this, your question is certainly understandable. The answer depends largely on the emotional maturity of the child. In our experience, most gifted children are able to handle early admission or advancement of one grade level with little, if any, difficulty. This does not mean that some problems will not arise. If your child is the smallest in the class, he will experience many of the difficulties that are associated with this. When he reaches teenage years, he will be the last child in his class to get his driver's license and may be noticeably smaller than the rest of the boys since they will reach puberty ahead of him. But in the "trade-off" of these problems versus those that accompany boredom, boredom usually results in more long-term disadvantages. Please understand, however, that this may not hold true for some school systems which are able to individualize their curriculum sufficiently with more than just a one or two hour per week "pull-out" enrichment class.

Double or triple promotion, though, needs more careful assessment. We would recommend that you consult at some length with educational and psychological professionals before taking such a step. Perhaps it would be better to have a single promotion with highly enriched outside experiences or special classes. Nevertheless, we do know of situations where a child with exceptional ability has run into a new "ceiling" again, even after a double promotion.

My school's psychologist says my child is gifted, but will not tell me her exact IQ score. Do I need to know this?

You probably do not need to know the exact IQ score, though it is helpful to know the range of eight or ten IQ points within which the score falls. This allows for the natural variation that occurs in most testing situations. Remember that there is an "optimum" range of intelligence — between about IQ 125 and IQ 145. Within this range the scores do not matter a great deal. The child is sufficiently bright to do almost anything she wants to do occupationally or otherwise. Beyond a score of 145, particularly as you get beyond an IQ of 160, some special planning will be needed, and thus you will need more information about the specific test results. Regardless of the overall IQ score, it is much more important for you to know what the test has shown regarding specific strengths and relative weaknesses. This will allow you to have more realistic expectations of your child, as well as discover ways to help her use her strengths to further develop those areas where she is less strong.

My child was not identified for the school's gifted program, but he seems to exhibit many characteristics of being gifted. Could the school have overlooked him?

Yes, it is quite possible that he is gifted, but not yet identified. You can check your impressions in several ways. Compare your child's abilities with those of children the same age; libraries have books with tables showing developmental schedules and milestones. Talk with your pediatrician or nurse about how your child's development compares. Talk with other parents, particularly parents of gifted children. You can have your child evaluated outside the school system by a qualified psychologist or school psychologist. If this confirms your impressions, treat your child as though he is gifted, and begin conversations with the school system to encourage them to take another look.

The achievement test scores show that she is functioning two grades above her current placement; but she is bringing home "C" and "D" grades on her report cards. Which do I believe — her grades or her achievement test scores?

For achievement, believe her test scores. She did not score that high by accident or by faking the test. It is likely that she is not showing her achievement in class for some definite reason.

Perhaps this is because grades are not important to her, because she does not want to reveal giftedness to her classmates, or because she is in some power struggle with her teacher or with you. Particularly for teenagers the desire for independence and to demonstrate self-control prompts them to attempt such power struggles. Given emotional support, courage and opportunity, she will eventually live up to her test scores in her day-to-day life. She will reach this sooner if school does not become a battle-ground.

"You may lead a horse to water, but you can't make him drink!"

English Proverb

"You can drive a horse to drink, but you can't make him water."

Margaret A. Munger

"Every human mind is a great slumbering power until awakened by a keen desire and by definite resolution to do."

Edgar F. Roberts

"Lack of something to feel important about is almost the greatest tragedy a man can have."

Arthur E. Morgan

CHAPTER IV

MOTIVATION

Underachievement in school is perhaps the most common motivational problem parents observe, though it is not the only one. When gifted children enter school, parents begin to be concerned about their children living up to their potential. During the preschool years they have demonstrated such enthusiastic curiosity that it is not motivation, but discipline, that is most likely to be of primary concern. While interrelated with motivation, discipline will be discussed in a later chapter.

The preschool gifted child most often fits the following self-descriptions (American Association for Gifted Children, 1978):

"I have this burning desire to learn!"

"I can remember having mad desires to learn how certain things worked, were put together; all from start to finish. Then I could know and at least be satisfied."

Why is it that so many gifted children suffer so wide a breach between potential and performance? What is it that causes so many gifted children to lose this spark? What can be done to rekindle it? How can the energy be channeled after it is rekindled? We hope this chapter will begin to unravel some of these questions, and will provide directions for parents and teachers.

Lack of Motivation

We assume you have already ruled out physical causes for underachievement — vision or hearing problems, a lingering infection, or (particularly in teenagers) malnutrition or drug or alcohol abuse. Convincing cases confirm the need to consider all of these conditions.

Next begin an inventory of the overall emotional status of the family. See if there are problems or crises that could be draining emotional energies so that little is left over for other accomplishments. Some commonly occurring crises include: recent or impending divorce or separation; family moves so frequent that they disrupt established friendships; frequent fighting, quarreling or other tensions within the family; disrupted relationships with his peers, siblings or dating partner. Realistically, there may be little parents can do to alleviate the stress of an unavoidable life situation. Even so, it is wise to weigh carefully the amount of pressure you might be adding by undue emphasis on achievement at such a time.

If emotional stresses, distractions and obstacles do not seem to be problems, and if your child is receiving as much support as you can reasonably provide, you must then consider how your child views her relationship with you and significant others around her. It is important to try to recall times when the child was particularly motivated — for what, and with whom. Discuss these situations with her and, through gentle questioning, let the child recall her feelings of worth and pride of accomplishment. Then you may wish to ask your child just to talk with you about why she seems so turned off (see the chapter on Communication of Feelings). Your goal is for your child to see herself as a person capable of worthwhile accomplishments and proud of it! If discussion and careful listening do not help, then you must explore some of the following areas.

Examine the models that you, the parents, provide for your child: What amount of time are you involved with your child? How encouraging are you? To what extent do you indicate that verbal expression is safe with you? How much do you convey your own eagerness to learn? All of these are related to your child's achievement and even to IQ scores.

Another place to look is, of course, the school situation. Perhaps this should even be the *first* place you look after you have examined your overall life situation. The normal gifted child enters school with an active curiosity about his environment and a tremendous urge to express himself and to relate himself to others. It is important to maintain his eager attitude, as well as to cultivate assertiveness and independence. Children who show such interest, curiosity and assertiveness as preschoolers have been found to obtain higher first and second grade achievement scores. The child's level of emotional independence from his teachers and his peers also predicts gains in achievement and in intellectual functioning even after second grade.

Many times, though, it can be difficult for that upper three percent of children called gifted to stay motivated in an educational system that is oriented primarily toward the other 97%. Too often the child's enthusiasm and motivation are stifled by persons more interested in seeing that he conforms to accepted patterns. Sometimes, in fact, it seems as if the teachers are in opposition to gifted children. It is not at all rare to learn of teachers who resent students who excel, who punish them with sarcastic remarks in class, or even with poor scores to "teach them a lesson." Other teachers express their discomfort by ignoring the gifted child, preferring instead to work with remedial students, perhaps to avoid being challenged by a child.

Not all teachers, however, punish or ignore gifted children, and many parents are able to keep their children motivated despite obstacles that ordinarily might reduce their motivation. These are those persons described earlier who "made a difference," whose characteristics are so central that they bear emphasizing. These persons encouraged participation, showed interest in the child's activities and feelings, allowed the child to share her discoveries and thoughts, avoided ridiculing her, and communicated understanding and acceptance of her feelings, as well as that it was important for the child to succeed.

The child who is ready to learn and who wishes to learn is the one who will learn, provided he has the emotional maturity and opportunity. The focus, then, must be on discovering what is blocking the child from becoming ready to learn. If he is emotionally discouraged and does not want to learn, then the efforts of others to educate him will be unsuccessful. You can perhaps force a child to sit in his room with his books, but you cannot force him to learn — as too many parents have discovered! Where schoolwork has become a battleground, the child will almost always win the battle of grades if he wishes — and the prolonged battle will only serve to delay self-motivation. The challenge is to help the child become motivated by helping him discover reasons why he might want to learn and through removing blocks that are interfering with his becoming motivated.

Some common reasons for lack of motivation in gifted children are summarized in Table 6. When you are confronted with a child's underachievement, consider these possible reasons.

You may be saying to yourself, "But that's not the way it should be! Can't these children simply realize that those reasons aren't good enough!" But, if they did realize all of these things, they would not have a motivation problem; perhaps it will help to approach it from another direction.

Table 6

Common Reasons for Lack of Motivation

- It's easier to drop out than to fulfill others' expectations.
- It's a coping behavior to get teachers and parents off his back.
- It's a way of rebelling where his parents cannot win if he goes on strike in a passive way.
- It avoids risk-taking since he can always say he did not really want to try, and thus can save his ego.
- It can help him gain acceptance from his less gifted peers.
- It can be an expression of depression, perhaps of feeling misunderstood.
- It can be a way to get others to help him and to give him the attention he wants.

Where to Begin

In helping another person become motivated, you must present ideas and tasks in terms of the needs of that person. You must begin by starting with the child's feelings as they are *at this time*, and remember that people act out of *their* needs, not yours. For example, perhaps to him it is more important not to risk failure; or he may "need" to see a teacher lose face in her attempt to control him. It is important for you to recognize how he figures that it is good for him to resist, withdraw, or refuse what others expect of him. Through gentle questioning and acknowledging his feelings, you can then help him become aware that he may eventually be defeating himself in ways that he really would not like.

A child who is engaged in a power struggle with a teacher, or even with parents, may be a child who has cast the school or teacher or the school/parent coalition as the "enemy," always trying to get him to do junk he considers worthless. Sometimes parents may then have to deal with school as a "necessary evil" that may include lots of "Mickey Mouse" work, but also as a place that can provide a child with specific things he wants — such as access to future education that will involve more personal choice and may relate more clearly to what he wants to do. This may be a tightrope walk for parents — trying to be neither too supportive of the schools nor too negative. Gifted kids often relate better to philosophical goals than to pragmatic, practical ones. Nevertheless, as a parent you may be put in the position of admitting to grave philosophical shortcomings in the educational system while trying to convince your child that there are practical considerations which must take priority.

What Drives Our Behaviors?

There is a hierarchy of needs described by Maslow (1954) which helps explain the development of most persons, and which may provide understanding for some of the reasons for your child's behavior. These are presented in order, from the most basic human need to the most advanced — a sequence that we see in human development from infancy to adulthood.

Physiological Needs. (Level 1)

If the child is hungry or very fatigued, these basic physical needs will be the most important motivators at that time. It is difficult to help a child focus on other important dimensions until these Level 1 needs are met. Peanut butter on a carrot upon arrival home may reduce hunger and allow the piano practice or homework to appear a great deal more attractive. Your gifted child, with her high energy level, may simply need more frequent nourishment.

Safety Needs. (Level 2)

Self-protection is the next step. If a child feels unsafe, whether physically or mentally endangered, obtaining safety and protection becomes primary. It is difficult, then, for a child to expend energy on learning math facts if he feels vulnerable, exposed and unsupported.

Belonging Needs. (Level 3)

When the child's physical needs are reasonably well met, and when she does not feel threatened or endangered, her motivation turns toward desires to belong and to be loved. Self-identity comes largely from the degree to which she feels she belongs to certain groups and is respected by them. She feels herself like them; this similarity then suggests that she is acceptable. Of course no reasonable person feels that she must "belong" to every group or be held in esteem by all people. However, until a child learns how to differentiate the groups that are important and valuable for her from those that are not, she will spend a great deal of energy pursuing a sense of belonging and esteem in ways that are misdirected and changeable.

Needs for Self-esteem and for Love. (Level 4)

As the more basic needs are satisfied and the child comes to feel more secure, his motivations begin to turn inward. He begins to place more importance on how he feels about himself, and worries less about how others would feel toward him if he were to disagree with them. His personal values become clearer. He begins wanting to actively reach out to the world — to invest his energies and desires in loving ways toward others. He rewards himself through his own value sytem.

Needs for Mental Understanding and Self-Actualization. (Level 5)

When the prior needs are reasonably met, a person focuses internally even more on issues of "Who am I?" "Am I free to make choices in this world?" "What are the most important parts of being human?" "How should one human treat other humans and tthe other organisms in this world?" The person becomes aware of potentials and powers within himself, and seeks to develop and actualize these potentials. Gifted children have a strong potential to reach this advanced level of motivation.

As a rule, the basic needs must be reasonably satisfied before one can move on to more advanced needs. If a significant problem or threat develops with one of the earlier and more basic needs, that need will emerge and take priority over everything else.

How to Transfer Motivation

You may be asking, "Yes, but how can we use this list? What are some practical things we can do?" If you have understood what has been said so far and related it to your own situation, you already have taken a very practical step. Although more will be said later in the chapter on Communication of Feelings, it is essential that you understand that your child is not *unmotivated* — he is just not motivated in ways that *you* want him to be! To change this means that you must communicate that you want to understand, that you care and can be trusted with feelings and concerns that may be quite sensitive ones.

After you have begun to establish trust and a sense of actively caring, and feel you have some notion of your child's viewpoint and desires, you can consider three key approaches toward achieving a transfer of motivation. These three approaches are: successive successes, goal setting, and personal relationships.

Successive Successes

In working with your child — whether he is motivated, partially motivated, or negatively motivated — you must use "successive successes" toward achieving the desired result.[4] This concept is quite important, and will be mentioned several times in the chapters to follow. In successive successes you initially praise, encourage, reward or reinforce *even the slightest movement* in the "right" direction. Then as the child becomes successful in this, you begin to reinforce only if there is further movement toward the desired behavior. In this way you go in numerous, but small, successive steps that gradually approximate the behavior you seek.

Remember that people develop in areas they find rewarding, and initially you may need to reward even the smallest progress, or perhaps just reward the trying. Your goal is to help your child realize that it is to her advantage or benefit to try to achieve something. This benefit could either be *extrinsic* or *intrinsic*. Of course it is often best if persons do things for the sake of doing them rather than just for some kind of external reward, but often it is necessary to start with that reward. Keep in mind that rewards do not include just physical things. A few kind words of admiration or encouragement, or an arm on the shoulder can be even more important than money or a token.

In motivating new behaviors, the rewards must be frequent enough to maintain the new behavior. This point requires emphasis since it is perhaps one of the most overlooked aspects of behavior. The frequency with which a reward is given is more important than the size of the reward. For example, five balloons or "smiley faces" given separately over time are far more effective than one batch of five given all at once.

Another common error is to wait too long before giving rewards or other feedback. Immediate consequences are the most effective. When you delay, you run a risk that your child will stop engaging in the behavior you are trying to reinforce. He

---

[4] Behavioral scientists usually call this "successive approximations."

may not even associate your reward with his behavior. We recognize that you cannot always be right there to reinforce your child's behavior. However do the best you can to be as prompt as possible. Even an interim token reward, if immediate, can help to bridge the gap. This token can be anything from a wink or a smile to a poker chip or a written "IOU — one special treat."

To remain motivated for a long-term goal — for example for an entire semester — is difficult, and requires support from others, particularly for a child. Yet as parents we often set tasks in ways that demand or expect immediate long-term compliance, such as "If you show me that you can do it for one entire month, . . ." The ability to work for long-term goals is something that is learned — it does not just occur by happenstance. It requires careful goal setting, as well as interim rewards for achieving short-term goals. It is important not only for you to give frequent small rewards, but also to help your child learn *to reward himself* for achieving these partial successes. These are "rest stops" along the way to the overall goal. "Along the way" rewards can be particularly important for gifted children the first time they encounter a task that really challenges them and demands sustained effort.

Goal Setting

Inappropriate goal setting may lead the child to think of herself as a failure. She may set her goal far too high, or far too low — or she may set a goal in such vague terms (e.g., to be "good") that she cannot clearly tell when she has reached that goal. Gifted children, like most others, must learn the skill of goal setting. They must learn to set tentative, attainable, short-term goals, as well as long-term goals. A written goal statement or contract, drawn up by the child, sometimes helps. Since gifted children so often do organize themselves around goals, this skill of goal setting becomes particularly important. The techniques for goal setting and values clarification are frequently taught to adults. The intellectual abilities of gifted children, however, allow them to comprehend and use these mental approaches early in life.

Goal setting usually leads to goal clarification, particularly in complex human situations. It is hard to set goals or to become motivated when you have competing motives. Particularly, the child may have difficulty choosing alternatives that would be desirable in the long-term as compared with those that have a payoff only in the short run. The gifted child may find it easier to resolve such dilemmas if he has learned some ways of classifying values and setting priorities. For example, he might find it helpful to play a conceptual game where he would consider what he would choose to do if he had only six months to live. What would he need in order to do this? How could he invest in himself so that he could do this? What would be the effects on others? How important is this for him?

Parents, too, need to examine their own values. As parents do you want your child to become valedictorian or president of the class, or are you more interested in whatever the child's unique *persona* and goals might create. Are your goals *as parents* practical? Are you wanting your child to settle on a profession that will pay well and provide security, or are your goals more philosophical — such as wanting your child to feel fulfilled. Or do you insist on both fulfillment *and* security? What intermediate goals have you set for your children? How will you be able to recognize when your child has reached one of these goals? Are you letting your goals inappropriately override your child's — perhaps trying to recapture a lost opportunity from your own childhood? As parents of gifted children, you particularly need to question your own needs for social approval, since that will have a huge bearing on how you and your children deal with the problems you encounter. Those of you who would like to delve more deeply into goal setting might wish to consult the book, *Values Clarification* (Simon, et al, 1972).

If goals are accompanied by the related necessary objectives, they become more attainable and the child is more able to see herself as successful. *How* are you going to get there? *What* do you need to do to accomplish this? *What time period* is allowed for this? What are your *criteria* for success? Breaking big goals down into necessary and attainable tasks helps give children a sense of control, and a feeling of competency will come from achieving these intermediate steps. This, in turn, fosters continued motivation and helps prevent discouragement.

Personal Relationships

The more personal meaning and emotional impact a task has, the more compelled we are to achieve it. Similarly, the more relevant knowledge is to personal relationships we enjoy, the more interested we are in acquiring that knowledge. Motivation to achieve, learn, display knowledge and contribute to a group is intimately related to how a child views himself and how he feels he fits in with significant others.

Most human needs are met directly or indirectly by our association with others, and most motivation or stifling of motivation in children occurs because of the behaviors of those around them. This characteristic of human existence provides you opportunities to positively influence your child's motivation by building upon your relationship with your child. There are several ways that you can share yourself with your child to help him become more motivated or to channel his motivation in different directions.

Recognize accomplishment. Express how *you* feel and how *you* interpret the child's feelings. It is all too often that we ignore the child, or label or evaluate him instead. For example, rather than "That was a good report card," you might say, "I feel very proud and happy when I see a report card like that. I imagine you are proud of your progress, too." These are the "I statements" that may be familiar to you from *Parent Effectiveness Training* (Gordon, 1970).

Encourage attempts. In talking about your behavior or the child's make it clear that you expect progress, not perfection. Convey a sense of trust that the child will act intelligently and responsibly.

Share an activity. When you and your child act together, your child can see *your* motivation at work, can develop an appreciation for your values, and can perhaps catch some of your excitement or sense of gratification.

It is difficult to discuss goal setting, successive successes and personal relationships separately. In most real life situations they are inextricably intertwined. All three are useful approaches toward achieving a transfer of motivation.

Remember gifted children almost always are motivated toward *something*. It is not that they are without motivation, but rather that their energies are not focused where you want them to be. Through personal relationships, successive successes, goal setting and other techniques, it often is possible to build from their existing activities to shape, transfer and channel their motivation. A high degree of achievement in one area usually will have a spillover effect, and help the child be motivated to achieve or learn in other areas.

Overachievement

Overachievement is something that we hear few parents complain about. It is more likely to be apparent as a problem in adult life. We are more and more aware of the "workaholic" who wakes up sometime in midlife to discover that he or she has never "really lived," that he has substituted work or achievement for every other human value. Parents, thinking of their job in terms of dealing with *children,* may forget to project into the future the values they are teaching their children to see how those values will affect adult lives. All people need to relax, to play, to take the time necessary for deep and satisfactory human relationships. Overachievement in gifted children can be the beginning of a major problem.

Where gifted children are unhappy with themselves or with their life situations, they often turn eagerly — even desperately — to achievement to fill the emotional void. To be the top person in a field usually demands that you make numerous personal sacrifices and show intense prolonged dedication. Parents of gifted children may find themselves consciously or unconsciously pushing their children — pointing out to them that they have the ability to be the best in their chosen areas. But at what expense? For too many gifted children, particularly as they become young adults, their high achievement is at the expense of developing mutually caring and supportive relationships.

Invest In Your Relationship

How can parents help their children become highly motivated, but still be content as people and intimately connected with others? The key, in our opinion, is a natural extension of the points we made earlier concerning underachievement. The seeds for overachievement are planted early. Achievement, rather than the person, is emphasized. This may be due to parents doting on his trophies, or because significant others place great emphasis on his accomplishments, or because he, himself, finds his achievements a refuge from unpleasant surroundings. The central underlying component to all of these, however, is that he has not been able to feel lasting acceptance of himself as a person.

In addition, the praises received by overachieving gifted children usually are of the "Yes, but . . ." type. That is, "You did well, but it would have been better if you had done it a different way." The repeated message is "You really aren't quite an acceptable person as you are — but if you just did a little more, perhaps you would be."

In practical terms, then, check how much emphasis you are putting on achievement at the expense of your relationship with your child. Examine your communications with your child; particularly see whether you would say these same things to adults you respect and enjoy. For example, would you really say to your spouse, "Honey, those pork chops were pretty good tonight, but you could do better than that if you only really put your mind to it." Or would you say to your husband or wife, "Sweetheart, if you only tried harder, you could surely fix this broken window as well as John, our next door neighbor. All you need to do is show a little more pride in your work."

In all too many of our attempts to motivate our children we convey that they are not quite good enough, and we chip away at their self-concept. We blame them because their judgment is not good enough, compare them openly and publicly with others, or indicate that their interests or behaviors are not good enough.

Our goal must be to help our gifted children develop their interests in ways that they find pleasant and exciting, and that they can share meaningfully with others. To guide this development requires discipline — particularly self-discipline — for both the child and his parents as part of developing a firm self-concept.

References

American Association of Gifted Children. *On Being Gifted.* New York: Walker and Co., 1978.

Gordon, T. *Parent Effectiveness Training.* New York: Peter Wyden, Inc., 1970.

Maslow, A.H. *Motivation and Personality.* New York: Harper and Row, 1954.

Simon, S.B., Howe, L.W. and Kirschenbaum, H. *Values Clarification,* New York: Hart, 1972.

Some Frequent Questions About Motivation

Even when I try to bribe my child, he will not cooperate. How can I make him do the things he should?

Bribes seem particularly ineffective with gifted children. They see through attempts at manipulation. A reward is different than a bribe. A bribe is part of a contract you are offering your child to try to induce him to do something that he does not want to do. He has the "right" to reject a contract that is offered this way. A reward on the other hand, is a pleasant offering that is not part of a contract. You may gain temporary conformity through force and setting limits, but to get cooperation you must generate a relationship of trust and a feeling of shared goals. This takes patience, time and skill to help your child see the importance of cooperation and the value of the things you want him to do with you.

If I give my child rewards, isn't it likely that she will grow up expecting rewards rather than doing some things just because they need to be done?

This is less a concern with gifted children than with many other children. Most gifted children seem intrinsically motivated; they are curious and find various activities enjoyable just for the pleasure of doing them. The problems usually arise when demands are made by others. Rewards are a way to begin shaping behavior or to teach new behaviors until those behaviors become enjoyable in their own right. It is important to realize that much of the world's energy is appropriately spent working to obtain rewards — only adults call it money. To have a predictable paycheck is a desirable goal. Some gifted children have the opposite problem; they are often uninterested in material rewards, and thus parents are often frustrated when they try to use rewards to make children conform to a usual work pattern.

My child seems to live in his own world. It doesn't seem to matter what we want him to do. How can we get him more involved?

It may create a bridge between you and him if he feels that what *he* does is important to you! You can begin by depending upon his abilities; let him give to you. When you allow him the pride of enriching you, you convey that what he has to offer is worthwhile.

My child could get all "A's" if she would only apply herself. Why won't she? What can I do?

She probably does not achieve because it's not that important to her, even though it is important to you. It is somewhat like getting your first car. Remember how unimportant expenses were to you when you were driving your parents' car? You did not worry about how much gas you used, or how much rubber you burned off the tires. But when you got your own car, things were suddenly very different! It *was* important to you! Find ways to relate your interests to her interests. What are the strengths you can build on? Your interest in her as a person and in her achievements are good places to start, along with a clear recognition and announcement to her that school is her responsibility and that you have confidence that she can manage it. (Actually, since you cannot force her to get better grades, you are not giving up any control — you never had it in the first place!) You can serve as a resource person to her by helping her think through what she might do about *her* problem: whether *she* would like to obtain a tutor or whether *she* would like to have someone listen to her recite. If she does decide on a tutor, she should call to set up the appointment; she should negotiate the fee within a certain range; and she should have the right to cancel appointments or to fire the tutor. You can provide transportation and part, or all, of the costs. This allows you to be free to be supportive, to praise and encourage her.

How do you channel motivation? My child wants to focus only on his astronomy — morning, noon, and night!

It sounds as if you have an excellent opportunity since you have a clear place to start! Now the challenge lies in building from the astronomy base to bring in other areas. Topics such as physics and mathematics will be relatively easy; English and political science may be more difficult, but it can be done. Remember to start where your child is in his interests, and to use his strengths so that the situation will work for him rather than against him. For example, you might help him become involved in writing or editing an astronomy newsletter, or in monitoring national legislation or international efforts which attempt to promote our space program politically.

"People seldom improve when they have no other model but themselves to copy after."

Oliver Goldsmith

"There is no such thing as a 'self-made' man. We are made up of thousands of others. Everyone who has ever done a kind deed for us, or spoken one word of encouragement to us, has entered into the make-up of our character and our thoughts, as well as our success."

George Matthew Adams

"To be in good moral condition requires at least as much training as to be in good physical condition."

Jawaharlal Nehru

"All of us have two educations: one which we receive from others; another, and the most valuable, which we give ourselves."

John Randolph

CHAPTER V

DISCIPLINE

What does discipline have to do with giftedness? Perhaps more than most people recognize. In this chapter we will focus on some particularly relevant aspects of discipline. First, it is vital to distinguish between "discipline" and "punishment." Punishment can actually decrease a child's measured intelligence. At least one study (McCall, et al, 1973) found that preschool children from homes where parents imposed severe penalties for misbehavior showed a significant decrease in IQ scores. This same study also showed that where parents were extremely lax in discipline, children lost IQ points during their preschool years, but then largely regained their previous IQ scores during middle school years. In contrast, children from families that gave them definite encouragement, stable structure, and reasonably consistent limit enforcement without being severe, actually increased their IQ scores up until age eight.

Discipline Is More than Punishment

Punishment is largely a negative term — a negative concept. Discipline, on the other hand can be positive. Discipline means teaching a child self-control so that he will ultimately be able to incorporate values and standards into his life in order to interact responsibly with others in predictable, mutually satisfying ways.

Discipline can be a loving pattern that helps your child learn alternatives. It is an opportunity for your child to discover and depend upon his *own* power.

The goal of discipline, then, is self-direction, while the goal of punishment is to impose direction from outside. Particularly for gifted children, self-direction is vital. The wants, needs, desires and interests of the gifted child are, in our experience, typically broader than those of the average child, and usually their motivation and involvement are more intense. Many parents have told us that their gifted children do not seem to know the meaning of the word "stop," they sometimes have difficulty behaving in calm, civilized, well-modulated ways. One parent said, "My child has two speeds — full ahead and stop — with nothing in between." We, too, have noted that for many gifted children it is as though their life motto is "Anything worth doing is worth doing to excess!" This intensity can be a great strength, but it can also be a child's undoing. He needs to develop tolerance both for his own limitations and the limited capabilities of others. To do this requires self-discipline and self-control.

Perhaps it will be helpful to review some basic principles of human behavior that will provide a foundation on which to base methods for shaping and modifying behavior which lead to self-discipline.

Almost everything a person does is motivated by some anticipated consequence, reward or pay-off. In most situations there are several consequences which serve to maintain a behavior — some positive, others not. For example, people go to work partly because they receive money, partly because of their own pride in accomplishment, and partly because others expect them to work. There is both implicit and explicit praise for the person who does work, and criticism of the person who does not. It is important to remember that both the praise and the criticism are reinforcers. While most people work to get praise and to avoid the criticism, there may be situations in which the criticism becomes the pay-off, as with the "drop-out" hippies of the sixties. Failing or disruptive behavior by children is usually as goal-oriented as is cooperative behavior directed toward success. The key to understanding it is in discovering the goal. In any case, actions that are reinforced tend to be repeated.

Since most behaviors are learned, they can also be modified. We have opportunities to help children to shape and control their own actions if we can avoid the temptation to impose control too completely from the outside. Because gifted children are so adept at learning, they can often quickly master ways of modifying their conduct. To achieve this they need suitable information and feedback.

Setting Limits

Clearly stated and mutually understood rules, limits and expectations for conduct give a sense of security and stability. This is particularly important for the younger child. The older child, hopefully, will have integrated her own values, limits and expectations into appropriate self-disciplined behavior. Limits help a child to be in control of herself and the situations around her.

All children need limits. Too often parents and other adults are afraid to set limits, or feel that they do not need to set limits for a gifted child. They seem to expect that a smart child can handle herself with good judgment. But even the gifted child lacks the experience on which to base good judgment. Being turned loose in a world without limits is like being turned loose in an unmarked mine field. The child never knows which step is going to blow up in his face — which action will pass unnoticed and which may bring down the wrath of the grownup world. He may feel that the adults around him would label the mines more clearly if they really cared for him. In such a dangerously limitless world, the gifted child may well spend a great deal of time and energy deliberately provoking explosions just to find where the mines are hidden. Clearly marking the limits of behavior, however, provides the gifted child with a secure area in which to behave as creatively as he wishes, and to develop himself up to those limits. Then he does not need to continually check to see where the boundaries are. Of course, the gifted child, like other children, will also go beyond the limits on occasion, sometimes just to see how powerful the explosion really is.

However, it is important to understand that gifted children may need fewer constraints than others. The boundaries we provide should allow room for growth and experimentation so that they are not perceived as prisons. Through experiencing and understanding natural and logical consequences, and through participating in defining the limits, gifted children learn much earlier than most children to set their own limits. As they learn by encountering the consequences of their actions, they are adding to their store of experience — the very experience needed as the basis of good judgment.

Breaking the Rules

It is necessary to consider enforcement, because the limits *will* be broken! Wherever possible, we recommend that natural consequences be allowed to occur — a principle we discuss more fully later on. The child who refuses to practice the violin according to an agreed-upon schedule, will have to face his teacher's distress or his own failure to play as well as he had hoped to at a recital. But sometimes it is necessary to impose our own disciplinary consequences.

When restrictions are imposed, they should be set firmly, consistently, and with a clear understanding of the reasons for them. Gifted children are usually more willing to comply with rules for which they see valid reasons than with rules they see as arbitrary or established only to exhibit adult power. Enforcing limits does not imply that you should be rigid. It does mean that you should *not* set limits that you really do not intend to enforce — at least when you cool down. For example, "You're not allowed outside of the house for any reason whatsoever for the next six months!" is an unenforceable restriction. The inconsistency inherent in setting a limit which you cannot or do not enforce weakens your credibility, undermines the importance of the limit, and makes it more likely that your limit will be tested again, unless the child understands good reasons why you withdrew the limit or did not enforce it. In such situations it may be wiser to renegotiate the situation. You can begin by saying, "I was thinking about what I said yesterday and I think that perhaps I need to make some changes in that limit."

The basic principle we are emphasizing is: *set as few limits as are really necessary; but where you set them, be consistent in following through.* Do not be surprised to have your limits tested, however. Gifted children are particularly curious to see if you will be consistent, and will really carry through with what you have said. Since they are highly verbal, gifted children often tend to argue and to logically defend their reasoning and viewpoint. You should expect this, and see this as a strength to be put to good use in establishing limits rather than as a threat to enforcement. Encourage your child to participate in developing limits for himself. Another strength that can be enlisted is the gifted child's ability to empathize with others. Wherever possible, show the child not only how a limit will affect him, but also how it is essential to the people around him.

Since the ultimate goal is self-discipline, encourage his opinion about how he will benefit from this restriction. Also remember that you and your child will need to re-evaluate your limits as your child develops new competencies — as gifted children are particularly likely to do. If setting limits has been a particular area of difficulty, you may wish to read some popular books by Ginott (1965; 1969) and Wright (1980).

Natural Consequences

Natural consequences are preferable to discipline imposed artificially or arbitrarily. We recommend that you allow natural consequences to occur wherever possible since the feedback from such situations is far more effective, as well as allowing you to preserve your relationship with your child. For example, if ten year old John forgets his lunch, the natural consequence is that he would become hungry — a consequence far more effective and meaningful than if mother brings him his lunch, along with a lecture. As the proverb says "The child who has burned his mouth, eats his soup more slowly."

This approach allows your child to discover consequences on his own — and allows you to adopt a role of supporter, encourager and commentator in a positive fashion. You are also able to avoid being caught in the middle of conflicts that are really not *yours*. For example, if your daughter decides that a school project is "dumb," it is neither appropriate nor helpful for you to attempt to rescue her by talking to her teacher. You may counsel her about alternatives she might wish to consider, but you should not intervene except in an extreme situation.

Natural consequences are not always negative ones, of course. However, parents are less likely to become involved unless there is a problem. We are not saying that this is how it should be; we are just recognizing how it appears. Positive natural consequences provide you with opportunities to help your child appreciate his competence, and to consider additional ways that he can use for achieving success. For example, when Sue reports that she has finally succeeded in getting "Mr. Mean" to smile, you might add a comment like "You really worked at that! I am impressed by how many ways you help people feel happy. Are there some other ways you have thought of, but have not tried yet?"

The natural consequences approach in child rearing has been presented clearly and eloquently by Dreikurs (1958; 1964). In addition to our summary here, we recommend that you read the excellent examples provided there.

Sometimes it *is* necessary to enforce your limits by imposing your own disciplinary consequences. You cannot, in some situations, allow natural consequences to occur because they are dangerous or otherwise inappropriate. Even though your intervention is not a "natural" consequence, it can be more effective by using the following guidelines for praise and punishment.

Again, it is important to remember the difference between discipline and punishment. Punishment only tells a child what *not* to do — not what *to* do. It usually evokes anger, resentment and sometimes revenge. Punishment also conveys that the source of control over his behavior and responsibility for behavior lies outside himself. Instead of learning to evaluate his own actions, he relies on adults to do that for him, and to decide the consequences of negative behavior.

Raise with Praise

In contrast to punishment, discipline usually involves positive reinforcement in addition to limit-setting and, perhaps, appropriate punishment. The goal is self-direction and self-regulation.

When most people think of discipline, they do not think of giving rewards. They should. One thing that we have learned from behavioral psychology is that rewards are vastly more powerful than punishment. Because of the sensitivity of gifted children, a little bit of punishment, whether it is verbal or physical, usually goes a long way.

Praise is a powerful reward, yet it is rarely invested in our relationships. Surprisingly, some parents have told us that, since they were not raised with praise, they do not know how to give praise. Others have felt that their words of encouragement were stilted and their repertoire was limited. Since gifted children enjoy variety, and since repetitions of a predictable response may make it ineffective, we have included a table of diverse phrases to help you convey fresh enthusiasm (Table 7).

We are *not* saying that you should always praise your child and that you should never punish him. Punishment may be the consequence of breaking an important rule, regulation or limit. But praise will be more influential in the long run, because the message you convey with praise is that the child is competent. The child who believes in his competence is able to begin taking the responsibility for his behavior.

Handle Feelings First — Discipline Second

When discipline problems occur, it is best to respond initially *not* to the particular *event,* but to the feelings that seem to surround it. If you handle the feelings first, then communication and learning can follow. It is extremely difficult for a child to be logical or to think clearly when he is experiencing a strong emotion. Further, recognizing the distinction between the feeling that motivated an action and the action itself helps the child recognize that distinction. Showing the child that you care about him and his feelings, also helps him believe that you and he are

Table 7

"Praises Phrases"

Thanks for helping.	Much better, keep it going.
That's worth a triple WOW!	BEAUTIFUL!
I'm proud of you.	You did very well. Nice going.
Truly an improvement; good!	Now you got it.
Terrific work!	Your comment is interesting.
Marvelous!	You made that look easy.
Very sharp. I'm impressed.	You are very good at that.
That's really clever.	You've just about got it.
You made a good point.	You are learning fast.
Out of sight!	You're getting better everyday.
You handled it well.	You really make my job fun.
Congratultions.	That was first class work.
SUPER! SUPER! SUPER!	FANTASTIC! WOW!
Very creative.	Well look at you go!
Truly great.	Thanks for working together.
Keep it up, you're doing fine.	Nicely done!
I like what you're doing.	Good effort.

I admire the way you keep trying.
You should be quite proud of yourself.
I hope you feel pleased about your work.
That looked very difficult to me.
Thanks for getting settled quickly.
I'm really pleased with your work.
You are very important to so many people.
I'm proud of the way you worked today.
It's a pleasure to see how courteous a child can be.
You do that well enough to help your sister learn
   how to do it.
You're such a joy to me!
I couldn't have done that without you!
I really appreciate how you help us.
You really planned ahead, didn't you.
Thank you for letting me watch you.
I appreciate your thoughtfulness.

allies rather than adversaries. Discipline is usually easier when your child feels that you are "on his side" and that he can be "on yours." Finally, the purpose of his misbehavior may well have been to have his feelings recognized and to validate that you really care about him.

Sometimes we over-emphasize discipline and neglect the importance of our relationship with our child. In doing so, we may achieve temporary conformity, but not lasting self-discipline stemming from the child's own values. And even that temporary conformity is bought at a cost. It is somewhat like the relationship recruits have with their First Sergeant; they conform to what he requires, but separate themselves from him at the first opportunity. In winning a power struggle or other confrontive situation, you may diminish a cooperative attitude or even jeopardize your entire relationship with the child. The price of victory may be a gnawing resentment.

Since gifted children are so often strong-willed, this important consideration must be kept in mind. They are especially susceptible to power-struggles because they are able to see several possibilities in any situation. If you present the situation as having a single possible solution — yours — with no room for question and no alternatives, you set the stage for a struggle in which one party wins and the other loses. The relationship between victor and vanquished is always more difficult than the relationship between allies who have solved a problem together. Nonetheless, we do recognize that there will be areas in your child's life in which your solution will have to be the one acted upon, regardless of the child's feelings.

Choices

Gifted children need choices and thrive on them. Choices provide children with opportunities to develop self-esteem and a sense of competency. Allow your child to choose in as many situations as possible. Too often as parents we make decisions for our children that they are quite capable of making themselves. Encourage your child to take responsibility for himself and his actions by pointing out options and by giving him choices. Just be sure that they are *real* choices. For example, do not ask your child whether she wants to get her tetanus shot. That is not a real choice since not getting it could endanger her life. Instead, ask her "Would you like your shot in the left arm or in the right arm?" That is a choice that she is allowed to have, and does provide some sense of control in the situation. Similarly, instead of asking her if she would like to clean up her room, you might say, "Would you like to clean up your room before your snack or after your snack."

The key is to give choices that are acceptable to you, rather than giving what appears to be a choice, only to take it back. By emphasizing real choices, you can prevent many confrontations that might result in win-lose conflicts, while at the same time promoting healthy independence and self-discipline. Most gifted children break their parents of the habit of casually using false-choice language by taking it literally — "Would you like to go up and brush your teeth now?" the parent says, and the child answers, "No." Instead of replacing this false-choice language with orders, try to replace it with genuine choices. By emphasizing the child's ability to choose, you can avoid many win-lose conflicts.

There is another kind of false-choice situation that puts a child into the position of loser, no matter what he chooses. Parents sometimes make their own preference abundantly clear, but may wish to avoid giving a direct order, knowing the child's strong preference is the opposite. They say instead, "You choose," and the child is left to risk their displeasure if he chooses as he really wants to, or to appear to freely choose what he really does not want. "You may come with us to visit Grandmother in the nursing home, or you may be selfish enough to stay home and goof around with your friends. Which will it be?" How is a child to deal with such a choice? If he chooses as his parents want him to, he dare not even grumble or complain, because "You did not have to come, you know; we gave you the choice!"

Some Helpful Techniques

In working with parents of gifted children, we have found the following suggestions quite helpful. They can be used within the framework of limits, natural consequences and choices.

Respond to the child's needs, not to his negative behaviors. By understanding the reasons for your child's behavior, you will be able to respond more constructively, and to avoid a reaction that could make the situation worse rather than better. Understanding the child's needs, however, does not mean that you necessarily must accept or even tolerate the behaviors. The goal of discipline is, after all, to help the child handle needs and feelings within the bounds of acceptable behavior. Sometimes behavior is motivated by conflicting feelings such as "I know it will embarrass me to criticize my teacher, but then I'll feel smarter and superior." Sometimes a discipline problem is the result of a child's feeling depressed or afraid. Your handling of the situation may be different if you are able to carefully perceive the feelings underlying the behavior, rather than just react to the apparent behavior.

Use "anticipatory praise." This is a particularly powerful technique with gifted children. In anticipatory praise, you praise what the child *may be about to do.* For example, when Johnny is just beginning to push back his chair from the table and dash out the door to play, you might say, "Thank you, Johnny, for taking your plate to the kitchen. I really appreciate your remembering to do that!" You may know perfectly well that Johnny never had that thought in mind, but your anticipatory praise does three things. First, it conveys to him your general expectation that he will behave in a responsible manner; second, it reminds him what he is supposed to do and praises (reinforces) him for doing it; third, it avoids a negative situation in which he would have been criticized had he dashed out the door to be called back.

Sometimes, of course, Johnny will say "I really was not going to take my plate to the kitchen." You still are ahead by using this approach since you have yet another chance. Now you can say, "Oh, I felt sure you were. Well, at any rate, would you please do so now?" Many a gifted child will see through the whole endeavor, of course, and the two of you may have a good laugh at how it worked out.

Put it in Writing. Writing notes can be another effective method of communication. In fact, it is often far more powerful than talking. Write a note to your child when he does something you feel good about. It need not be long or elaborate, just a slip of paper left on his pillow. Such notes are particularly effective as reinforcers because they are concrete, collectible, completely individual and personal. You may also wish to write a note about how you feel about a particular negative behavior. Written communication allows the child to reflect before being required to respond to your comments. There is time for the child to think about his behavior without the pressure of a face-to-face confrontation. If you ask for a written reply, the child must face the responsibility of reasoning out his own alternatives.

Praise or punish the behavior rather than the child. Consequences are more effective when they are directed to a behavior, rather than to the child as a person. "You do that well" is generally better received than "You surely are a gifted (or talented, skillful, etc.) person." Similarly, it is preferable to disapprove of a child's behavior without sweeping attacks which criticize the child as a person. "Mary, actions like that are not allowed here," is much better than "You are an inconsiderate rule-breaker, and I have had it with you!"

Encourage your child to express how he feels. If this is done frequently, your child is more likely to feel that her views are important, and you will be less likely to have to deal with an explosion of accumulated anger and resentment. Allowing grievances to accumulate for long periods is like trying to store more and more things in a bag — it may be able to hold a lot, but eventually it gets so full that it breaks, everything spills out at once, and you have a real mess!

Express your feelings in various situations, whether you are encouraged or discouraged. It is often more effective to explain how you feel than to convey your judgment of his behavior from your superior position as parent. For example, "I feel very sad, surprised, and disappointed when you do not listen to other people," rather than "You were rude and irritating." Expressing your own feelings also gives permission by example, for your child to express his. In recognizing accomplishments, you also can express how *you* feel and how *you* interpret the child's feelings rather than labeling or evaluating him. For example, "It makes me happy to see you solve that puzzle," rather than "You are a genius!"

A written study or goal schedule, particularly if developed by the child, helps to discipline his school and home responsibilities. Young gifted children seem notably responsive to charts with stars or other tangible symbols of progress. Tokens of success provide powerful "along the way" rewards.

Use a "behavioral contract." Sometimes with older gifted children a disciplinary situation gets unusually complex. They may want to consider numerous aspects in complicated ways. Some parents have had success in asking the child to draw up a behavioral contract which spells out the expectancies and the consequences under various conditions. A draft of a contract may then become the starting point for discussions which lead to agreement. The experience of drawing up a contract that is fair to all parties is beneficial to a gifted child, and places direct responsibility upon the child for his behavior. Such a contract, tucked away in a drawer, also helps protect the parties involved against lapses in memory concerning the terms of the agreement.

Examine your expectations of your child. Are some discipline problems you are having due to your expectations which may not be appropriate to a gifted child in today's world? Most of us have expectations remaining from our own upbringing that do not necessarily apply now. Do you really *need* to have that particular behavior, or do you feel you must demonstrate your power and control? Are you afraid that if you give in, he will take over? If it is just a power struggle over who is in control, have you left your child a face-saving way out? How much are you replaying what you heard from your parents in your own childhood that did not work with you as a child, and probably will not work for you as a parent with your own children? If we were raised with the motto, "Children are to be seen and not heard," for instance, we need to decide whether we believe that motto or whether we are merely acting as though we do.

The wide variation in age-related behavior of gifted children can also lead you to expect too much from them. You may come to rely on the maturity they show in some areas, and demand that maturity at all times and in all areas. It is sometimes helpful either to observe other children of the same chronological age to remind yourself of "normal" behavior, or to reread one of the books outlining normal child development. It is unreasonable for parents to punish a seven year old for being a seven year old, even if at most times the child seems more like a ten year old.

Be clear about your expectations. Because many discipline problems come from misunderstandings, make unmistakeably clear what you expect your child to do or to not do. We often expect gifted children to read between the lines, and to just "know" what we want them to do. Sometimes this is true, and sometimes it is not, particularly if the child is preoccupied with some project of his own or lost in his own thoughts. We have found it helps to have the child repeat to you what you expect him to do. As he does, you may discover that he really did not hear you or did not understand the message the first time. Try again, and have him repeat it back until it is clear that he understands what you expect and what the limits are. A conversation might go like this:

Mom: "You may go to the hobby store, but you must meet me here at 4:00. Do you understand?"

Son: "Ummmm."

Mom: "Now, what did I say to you?"

Son: "That I could go to the hobby store."

Mom: "Almost. You can go the hobby store, *but* you must meet me here at 4:00. Now, tell me what you heard me say."

Son: "Aw, Mom! I have to be back here at 4:00 after I go to the hobby store."

Mom: "Bingo! I appreciate that. It's important to me that you understand what I said."

Touch your child. Another technique to avoid misunderstandings is to touch your child when you talk with him. Put your hand on his arm or around his shoulder. This focuses his attention and helps to insure that he really hears what you are saying. Use this same technique when you are setting or enforcing a limit with your child. The physical level of touching reinforces the limit you have set, while at the same time it conveys that you care about him and are an ally.

Convey your trust that your children will act wisely. To do otherwise indicates that you lack respect for them and their abilities; it also undermines their evaluation of themselves. Gifted children particularly need to learn to trust their own evaluations, and they can do this better if they feel parents trust *them.* Even though you may have to express distrust about their abilities on certain occasions, continually show them that you trust them as persons. Indicate clearly to your child that you value his independence, support his control of his own behavior, and hope he will become increasingly less dependent upon imposed discipline for his life style. Teach him creative problem-solving and decision-making techniques. Encourage him to be in charge of his own discipline so that he can increasingly feel that his destiny is largely by his choice, and that he is not just a piece of flotsam on the sea of life going wherever the waves take him.

Encourage gradual steps. Remember that self-discipline is learned. When a person learns anything new, he usually is clumsy with it at the beginning, and only gets better with practice. You will need to recognize and encourage *gradual* changes that are steps toward self-discipline.

Some Things to Avoid

In discipline it is important to know what *not* to do, as well as what to do. Certain approaches may only lead to problems, particularly with gifted children.

Do not use a child's strength for punishment. Avoid using your child's strength as part of your criticism of her. To do so makes it a disadvantage to have special talents. For example, saying to a child "If you're so smart how come you can't remember to take out the garbage," conveys to the child that she could avoid criticism by not being intelligent.

Another strength that is sometimes used against gifted children is their honesty. If your child tells you the truth, do not use it to punish, tease or embarrass her. Do not torment her with her honesty, and particularly do not bring up the event weeks or months later. If you punish her for trusting your understanding and compassion, it is not likely to encourage cooperation and truthfulness. Be alert to putting your child in the no-win position in which she gets punished if she is caught lying, but also gets punished if she is honest with you.

Avoid being a dictator. Authoritative demands for immediate action by the child are inconsiderate and should be avoided. All too often we have heard parents say to their child, "I don't care what you're involved in! We have to go *now!*" Since gifted children are likely to be involved in something *any* time parents want them to do something else, impatience builds. Giving the child a warning about *when* you wish to leave allows him to arrange to get to a stopping point. It is the way we would communicate with an adult whose respect we valued. "We need to go in about fifteen minutes; can you arrange to be finished by then, or can you find a good place to stop?"

"Doomsday threats" and "personal wipe-out statements" should also be avoided. A doomsday threat is one that virtually promises the end of the child's existence if he does not meet your demands. Not only do such threats prove ineffective, they are so exaggerated that they damage your credibility with the child in the future. Wipe-out statements are similarly exaggerated. These are statements like "You are always inconsiderate!" or "You never think of anyone but yourself!" These statements usually involve "always" or "never" and constitute a sweeping attack on the child's total character. These have no reasonable place in discipline. Not only are they ineffective, they are also harmful.

Do not use ridicule or sarcasm. Ridicule is likewise harmful. Gifted children are quite sensitive to ridicule and sarcasm, and easily hurt by it. When they are exposed to it, despite their own hurt, they sometimes begin using ridicule and sarcasm as weapons in their dealings with others — often with disastrous effects.

Avoid nagging your child or being nagged by her. The verbal skills of gifted children lead them to rely heavily on words, and they may be incredibly persistent in their demands. Their single-mindedness can prompt adults around them to drift into a tolerance for nagging. Dreikurs (1964) spells out an effective technique for this that we endorse. It is called "taking the sail out of the wind." If you are being nagged (or catch yourself nagging), turn on your heel without comment or explanation and go into the bathroom and lock the door. Keep the bathroom stocked with reading material to çalm you. Enjoy your reading until the nagging (or pounding at the door) has stopped. If the nagging begins again when you emerge, go back again, without comment, to the bathroom. Repeating this a few times usually proves to be effective in reducing nagging and useless bickering.

Have you drifted into a pattern of continually picking at your child for little, irritating behaviors? Periodically check yourself on this to see if you are harassing your child ineffectively. Instead of continually criticizing, learn to ignore the behaviors until they go away, or change your attitude about them, or do something *effective* to change them — but do not just continue to nag.

Do not let temper tantrums or other misbehaviors cause you to do what is self-defeating for you or for your child. This can be difficult. As the saying goes, "When you're up to your knees in alligators, it's difficult to remember that your objective was to drain the swamp." Nonetheless, continue to remind yourself of the need to maintain a sense of perspective about the goals you hope to achieve and the progress you have made.

Gossiping hurts. Many parents are careful to avoid gossiping about adults, but are not aware that they are gossiping about their children — often right in front of them. Usually this talk

102

involves a problem the child is having. We feel that it is as unfair
to a child as it is to an adult to air his problems in public, and can
set the stage for a discipline problem to get even worse. Our children understand the conversations they overhear on the phone
or with neighbors. Later, they may have difficulty seeing why
they are forbidden to talk outside the family about the parents'
marital problems!

Avoid harsh, inconsistent punishment. It is one of the most damaging approaches to discipline, as well as being ineffective in
changing most behaviors. Such punishment results in anger, distrust and disrespect for authority, and a feeling that the world is
unpredictable and unsafe. Children raised in such an environment rarely have an adequate self-concept or positive view of
themselves, and harsh, inconsistent punishment fosters delin-
quency or even criminal behavior (McCord, et a., 1959).

References

Dreikurs, R. *The Challenge of Parenthood,* N.Y.: Duell, Sloan &
Pearce, 1958.
Dreikurs, R. and Soltz, V. *Children: The Challenge.* N.Y.: Haw-
thorn Books, 1964.
Ginott, H.G. *Between Parent and Child.* N.Y.: Avon, 1965.
Ginott, H.G. *Between Parent and Teenager.* N.Y.: Macmillan Co.,
1969.
McCall, R.B., Appelbaum, M.I. and Hogarty, P.S. Develop-
mental changes in mental performance. *Monographs of the
Society for Research in Child Development,* 1978, 39 (3) (Serial
No. 150), 1-83.
McCord, W., McCord, J. and Zola, I.K. *Origins of Crime.* N.Y.:
Columbia University Press, 1959.
Wright, L. *Parent Power: A Guide to Responsible Childrearing.*
N.Y.: William Morrow and Co., 1980.

Some Frequent Questions About Discipline

You emphasize self-discipline. Should that not carry over into completing projects? My child starts a hundred projects and never completes more than a few. How do I help him achieve the self-discipline to finish what he starts?

Many parents of gifted children share your concern. We can reassure you, though, that in most cases self-discipline will come — along with maturity. It may help you to remember that many projects are not worth finishing, that some projects turn out to be beyond the child's capabilities and may be put aside until later, and that some projects provide enough challenge or learning or stimulation to the child in the early stages, so that completion is not really important. As a friend recently said, "Anything that is not worth doing, is not worth doing well." The world of gifted education may put far too much emphasis on "products" that are not worth doing, particularly with pre-teen gifted children. We may need to examine our own expectations; the self-discipline may exist, but not in ways we want. Many times a gifted child persists despite frustrations or obstacles to complete a project — proving he *can* persist when he wants.

There are, indeed, gifted children who really give up when anything becomes difficult or temporarily dull. Usually these are discouraged children, perhaps even depressed, who often expect criticism. You might wish to review some of the points raised in the chapter on Motivation.

Sometimes I feel like I've had it in trying to get my child to become civilized! When can I expect to see improvement?

It is understandable that sometimes you wish you had a placid or even dull child. The curiosity, energy, questioning, and ability to see and do things differently can add up to a very trying situation. Keep your courage! Virtually all gifted children do become "civilized" even though they may continue to march to a different drummer. As a matter of fact, most gifted children show a far greater concern for the welfare of humanity than most "civilized" persons — but they have little tolerance for useless conformity. Fortunately gifted children are usually quite capable of reasoning and anticipating probable consequences of situations. You can lighten your burden considerably by helping her develop the ability to learn how she would feel, how others would feel, and what would probably happen if she acted in a particular way. With this perspective, she can creatively explore options and expand her behaviors in ways that she decides reflect how she wants to be known.

When I discipline my child, she becomes a "Philadelphia lawyer" who argues about every loophole that I neglected to specify. Is this typical of gifted kids? How do I handle it?

Yes, this is typical, and takes much patience on your part. As much as possible, try to get her to appreciate the spirit and intent of the discipline, rather than focusing on the letter of the law. The more she understands the purpose of the discipline and the caring which lies underneath, the less likely she is to need to weasel through loopholes. Remember also, however, that most children test the limits with adults to find out where those limits are; this is a way of reassuring themselves that limits really do exist. It may also help to have her work with you in establishing discipline, including imposing punishments on herself should these be needed. Other parents have had their young "Philadelphia lawyer" draw up written contracts or agreements, in draft form, to provide a basis for discussion and to use this lawyering to advantage. Overall, the key here is patience and tolerance!

My gifted child says school is so "dumb" and that he can learn it on his own. He feels he knows more than his teachers, and his classes are so boring. I'm afraid he's going to drop out.

Many gifted children do drop out, but hopefully yours will not be one of them. This is a discipline problem that will not likely respond to punishment. It may respond to a combination of praise, encouragement and natural consequences. It is important for your child to know that you understand his feelings of frustration. You will need to avoid automatically siding with the teacher. Raise gentle questions with him about what *he* could do about *his* school problems, and whether he has suggestions about ways you could help him with *his* problems. Convey to him your sense of confidence that he, with your help, has the ability and discipline to meet with whomever is appropriate in the school system to develop ways for school to be less boring and more stimulating.

All of this notwithstanding, he may still drop out. Should this happen, you can help by letting natural consequences occur. Encourage him to experience living completely on his own, while at the same time maintaining open lines of communication. The self-discipline required in supporting oneself and coping with day-to-day problems often helps a person to see the relevance of school, as well as to develop a better sense of self-sufficiency and self-confidence. Fortunately, most gifted children get turned on occupationally at some later point in life, find themselves, and make up for lost time.

"Remember, happiness doesn't depend upon who you are or what you have; it depends solely upon what you think."

Dale Carnegie

"Men are not worried by things, but their ideas about things."

Epicetetus

"Nothing is so wretched or foolish as to anticipate misfortunes. What madness it is to be expecting evil before it comes."

Seneca

"Archie doesn't know how to worry without getting upset."

Edith Bunker

"He who has a why to live can bear almost any how."

Friedrich Nietzehe

CHAPTER VI

STRESS MANAGEMENT

As we noted in the first chapter, gifted children are subject to some stresses which differ from those of the average child. Since most people assume that gifted children have everything going their way, they often overlook the fact that these children are experiencing stress and need help. Granted, the amount of stress experienced varies with each child's temperament, and some children seem naturally to be calmer and less upset by situations. Even so, gifted children are likely to experience stress in various situations from feeling out of place with their environment.

Feeling out of step with family and friends is partly relative and partly absolute, depending on the surroundings. A child with an IQ of 130 or 140 is not likely to feel out of place in a small university town where there are lots of children of professional parents, although he might in an average or below average environment. Minority gifted children in ghettos may be so different from their environmental companions that they bear a special psychological burden. For the exceptionally gifted child, a certain amount of stress is virtually an absolute. The child with an IQ above 160 is likely to have difficulty fitting in anywhere — and must endure the stresses that accompany this. These children frequently have described to us the feeling that they are aliens in virtually all settings.

Learning to Tolerate Frustration

It is paradoxical that stress should arise because of their strengths — learning and acquiring skills quickly. This ease of accomplishment may lead to idleness and daydreaming, and can condition gifted children to habitually expect an effortless existence. At some time, though, gifted children do encounter unfamiliar challenges, at least in the form of discipline and the expectancies of others. Perhaps they discover problems in life that do not have solutions — only decisions or compromises. These dilemmas often come as a shock to them, and cause significant stress.

It is important for all children to develop a tolerance for frustration and stress. It is this stress tolerance that allows them to become persistent in their efforts and to tolerate the ambiguities of life. You can help develop your child's tolerance for stress and frustration by gradually exposing him to progressively more challenging situations — but ones he can handle. His increased accomplishment helps him realize that he can cope with difficult situations, and that it is not catastrophic if he must face a problem he cannot solve immediately.

Some Challenge Is Desirable

All of us need a certain amount of stress in our lives, though the amount varies from person to person. Too little challenge and we do not use our abilities to achieve sufficiently to feel worthwhile or important. Too much stress, and we suffer in one way or another. The stresses of challenge can be quite positive, and meeting goals we have set for ourselves can be enjoyable. If there are no goals, there can be no satisfaction of achievement, and a person's sense of worth may be undeveloped or reduced. It is important to help your child understand this balance so that she can establish goals that are appropriate, along with intermediate subgoals.

As many teachers, athletic coaches and others will tell you, kids do not know what they can do until they are challenged and become motivated. A key part of this, as will be discussed subsequently, is for the child to develop appropriate ways of appraising challenges and evaluating herself. When the mechanisms for maintaining self-respect and self-esteem are outside of yourself, then distress is more likely to result.

Burdensome Stress

In addition to the challenging stress noted above, gifted children may drift into particular areas of stress that are unproductive, but which they must cope with nevertheless. Many of these stresses stem from a combination of factors: the myths others believe about them, the sensitivity of these gifted children, their high aspirations, and the difficulty they may have in fitting in with peers, siblings and others.

Their social consciousness and alertness may cause these children to see numerous ways in which things could go wrong, or may prompt them to worry about abstract or remote problems. They often express concern with problems such as world hunger, the unequal distribution of wealth, and the high divorce rate, as well as with their own personal or family concerns. They are keenly aware of problems at a young age, yet may feel overwhelmed by a sense of helplessness since they are also sensitively aware that they are "just children."

The differences between the gifted child's moral and intellectual views and those of the others with whom he spends time can be a major stressor. The gifted child's perception of reality differs from the average child's perception of reality, and his concern with universal laws and principles rises above the usual provincial and personal ethical concerns of most people. Your child will likely need help in learning to lessen the inner tensions that arise from these differences between himself and others.

When a child exhibits unusual abilities, others tend to magnify them. They begin to see her as extraordinary, and as able to solve a wide array of problems. Their expectancies of her become exaggerated, and they may begin to expect perfection — that she can solve all problems. The gifted child's performance clearly does not reach this level, and as time passes the disparity between expectation and performance can be a great source of stress.

Emotional and Intellectual Maturity

It is difficult for parents and others who work with gifted children to remember that their emotional maturity may not be at the same level as their intellectual maturity. Intelligence is not the same as wisdom. Although he may know many facts within some area of life, the child's emotional maturity and judgment may not be developed to the same degree. This is not to imply that gifted children have poor judgment. Usually their judgment is well above average. Their intellectual abilities are even more advanced, and this discrepancy may lead to problems.

A gifted child may react emotionally in ways that are more appropriate to her age than to her intelligence — sometimes causing considerable consternation and confusion to her parents and others. If a child uses big words and advanced concepts, should she not be able to handle emotionally complex situations? Not necessarily! As Hollingworth (1975) noted, "To have the intelligence of an adult and the emotions of a child combined in a childish body is to encounter certain difficulties." That child may be able to speak eloquently about genetic transformations or computer memories during the day, but may still need her "blankie" to sleep with at night. Adults often do not understand, and may react with "If you're so smart, why do you have to act like such a baby?"

Managing Yourself

Other stresses are placed on gifted children by the insensitive behavior of others. Sometimes others act out of jealousy, resentment or lack of understanding; other times they seem to act out of foolishness. It will be important for you to help your gifted child learn to recognize that the behaviors and attitudes of others are largely outside of his control, but that he *can* control his own actions and reactions — a powerful tool for managing stress. With his self-management he can learn to cope with others and even to tolerate and enjoy them.

There is often a fine line between being polite to others and passively accepting stressors that others attempt to place on you. The difference is in how an individual has learned to think about the situation with which he is confronted. Because most children, even gifted ones, have a limited repertoire of responses for coping, the easiest way for them to resolve conflict may be to give up politely. They need encouragement and assistance in learning how to conform when necessary, but without giving up.

Self-Talk

In our work with gifted children and their parents, we have developed more appreciation for the importance of mental process which we call "self-talk," particularly as it relates to stress management. Self-talk is what we say to ourselves about ourselves — how we evaluate ourselves and what we do. Most people are aware of this at some time or other such as when they say to themselves "I really did lousy there." or "I'll never be able to do it" or "I'm just no good." Sometimes it is obvious to others that someone is "down on himself," "kicking himself around the block" or is "being too hard on himself." However, few people are aware that they are always talking to themselves mentally, and evaluating what they are doing, thinking or feeling.

Gifted children are particularly likely to engage in self-talk at an early age — much earlier than most adults around them realize. Because of a gifted child's high verbal and conceptual abilities, it is not uncommon for a gifted child to be evaluating herself via self-talk by age two or three, and to be putting these thoughts clearly into words. Thoughts that a two year old innocently expresses aloud will be kept to herself as she grows older.

Because of their perfectionism, gifted children are overly critical of themselves — that is, they engage in negative self-talk. They often are discontent with their behavior anytime it falls short of their personal goals, and they often experience feelings of inadequacy or inferiority as a result (Strang, 1951; Whitmore, 1980). Unrealistic expectations of themselves about what they "should" be able to do are often combined with unrealistic goals about task complexity. Sometimes, too, adults around them add to the pressures by demanding consistent excellence. Even if they can achieve at high levels, gifted children still are likely to be overly self-critical. Gifted achievers as well as gifted under-achievers suffer from feelings of inadequacy, and engage in a great deal of negative self-talk (Whitmore, 1980).

Negative self-talk is particularly stressful, and perhaps that is why we are often aware of criticizing ourselves. Most of us are less aware that we also have positive self-talk, and that we can buffer, support and reinforce ourselves by telling ourselves what a good job we did, or how proud we are of ourselves. Because of its importance to gifted children, and because it can result in stress, we will focus on self-talk in some detail.

Our stressful self-talk stems primarily from values, conflicts and emotion-laden appraisal regarding how others view us and what we "should" be doing, thinking or feeling. We spend a great amount of our time worrying about what is important to others because we want to be liked and do not want to appear noticeably different. At other times we are afraid to act on our ideas because we might fail, thereby proving to ourselves that we are less than we thought we were. We find we are not living up to our image of ourselves as we feel we should.

Irrational Beliefs

The most stressful self-talk is that which stems from irrational beliefs which then lead one to adopt inappropriate "should" attitudes. The more common of these unreasonable beliefs are summarized in Table 8. When viewed in the present context, these beliefs can be seen to be an unreasonable basis for our actions or self-evaluations. In day-to-day life, however, we often rely on these beliefs in our thoughts and actions, and fail to recognize how irrational, inappropriate and stressful they are.

Although most people at some time or other act on the basis of these irrational beliefs, the gifted child is particularly vulnerable to these traps because of his striving for achievement and perfection. Thus he must be taught to be aware of these beliefs, and to actively question his self-evaluations to see if he is setting unreasonable expectations for himself. It is important to help the gifted child learn *not* to base his self-talk on these hidden "should" statements. If no one points them out, he is likely to unknowingly adopt this belief system early in life, allowing it to become deeply ingrained. Undue stress, lack of self-acceptance, and feelings of anger, frustration, and even rage toward the world may result.

Table 8

Some Major Irrational Beliefs[5]
— You must be loved and approved of by everyone.
— You must do perfectly in all respects.
— A person who acts badly is a bad person.
— It is terrible, horrible, awful and catastrophic when things aren't going the way you want them to.
— Your happiness is caused by other events or people rather than by how you think or talk to yourself.
— If something is unpleasant, you should be preoccupied and continually upset over it.
— Things that have happened in the past are all-important, need to be continually worried about, and limit your possibilities for the future.
— People and things should be different from what they are, and it is catastrophic if perfect solutions cannot be immediately found.
— Behaviors that worked for someone else, or which formerly worked for you, are what must be followed.

Once aware of these irrational beliefs, these children can then begin to appreciate the effects of self-talk. You can help them understand that it is not the events that are stressful — it is what they tell themselves about the events that produce stress! Although they cannot control the behaviors of others, they can control their reactions and feelings toward others. More elaborate discussions of self-talk, irrational beliefs and how to manage them can be found in Ellis and Harper (1975).

---

[5] Adapted from A. Ellis and R.A. Harper, *A New Guide to Rational Living.* N.Y.: Institute for Rational Living, 1975.

Some Specific Suggestions

In addition to educating the gifted child about self-talk and possible underlying irrational beliefs, several specific steps can be taken to help her learn to manage stress better. As you read through these recommendations, please note that they build upon the principles outlined in the chapters on Motivation and on Discipline, such as successive successes and giving choices. We believe that stress management is a specific instance of self-discipline and plays a major role in motivation.

Covering up problems usually creates stress; talking about them generally helps. Denying difficulties or pretending they do not exist is usually more detrimental to gifted children than honest acknowledgement, discussion and reasoning. It helps to come directly to grips with stressful situations even though your child may be reluctant to discuss his feelings or to listen to other's feelings. Most stressful situations must be confronted before they can be solved, even if that confrontation temporarily intensifies the stress.

When a child is in a stressful situation and is caught up in irrational self-talk, it usually is not helpful to try to pointedly confront him about this. To do so only adds to his stress. Instead, encourage him to think aloud and share his stress with you, while you reflect his feelings. In particular, you can gently raise questions about "What is the worst thing that could happen in that situation?" and "How catastrophic would that be?" You can also reflect with statements like, "You feel you *should* . . ., but it sounds as if that is not what you want." Gifted children can quickly regain their sense of perspective, and reduce their level of stress.

Teach your children tools for making decisions. In some ways these techniques are similar to the values clarification exercises mentioned in the chapter on Motivation. In their simplest form, problem solving techniques involve: (a) defining the situation and the priorities, (b) defining the problem in terms of what needs to be done, (c) listing all of the possible solutions to the problem, (d) gathering information about the possible solutions, (e) evaluating the feasibility of those possibilities, and (f) making the decision. A step-by-step approach will help him see that most problems have many solutions that are within his control, although few solutions are perfect.

Another widely used problem solving approach is SCAMPER (Eberle, 1982). This method helps children break out of rigid thinking patterns that may cause them to view problems as insoluble. The acronym SCAMPER is an abbreviation for the following component steps in processing ideas and mental images for creative problem solving:

S . . . Substitute (What similarities exist; what could be substituted?)

C . . . Combine (Might something be combined or brought together?)

A . . . Adjust (What changes or adjustments could be made to help?)

M . . . Magnify, Minify, Modify (What could happen in these conditions?)

P . . . Put to other uses (In what other ways might parts be used?)

E . . . Eliminate, Elaborate (What could be removed or enhanced?)

R . . . Reverse, Rearrange (What effects would come from changing the sequence?)

As another part of problem-solving, teach them to set *short*-term, intermediate objectives, as well as long-term goals. As noted earlier, struggling to reach a distant accomplishment is stressful. For gifted children this can be particularly true since they so often over-schedule themselves. It helps them gain perspective if they can solidify their plans through developing a written plan of their goals, objectives, and a specific plan of action.

Help them reward themselves for their attempts at success as well as for achieving success. One specific goal should always be to "try again." Mistakes and failures need to be used as stepping stones to accomplishments, rather than as triggers for blame or depression. A failure can be a "successful" one. Encourage your child to adopt this view. When something fails, at least she knows more than she did before — now she knows what did not work. She can analyze why she did not achieve her goal, and use this awareness to work for her another time.

Blaming others is not helpful for reducing stress. It usually leaves the blamer feeling helpless since it depends upon someone else's actions. That is, the blamer is implying "I could be terrific if only you would get your act together." There is nothing you can do to improve a stressful situation if you are just waiting for someone else to change; thus blaming immobilizes you. It is important to help children discard the idea that they are passive, helpless victims who are unable to be creatively assertive.

Teach them that a problem situation often can work for them, rather than against them. If they think creatively, perhaps there are ways of using the situation to achieve some goal that is not immediately apparent. For example, when faced with being "stood up" by a date, can he use the time to go to the movie he has been wanting to see instead of moping, blaming and mentally making himself miserable so that he ruins the entire evening and perhaps the next day as well? Even in problem situations he has choices — whether to continue to dwell on his discomfort, or to put it behind him so he can begin once again to function effectively.

Compartmentalized thinking can be developed. Just because one area of your life is distressed does not mean that all areas of your life must be affected. With practice, gifted children and their parents can learn to limit their distress and concern primarily to those areas directly affected.

Immediate calming techniques are helpful. People who are in crisis or under acute stress often get so caught up with feelings of tension, fear or anger that they cannot think clearly. It is difficult to develop a plan for coping when you are overwrought emotionally. Though children are often told to "calm" themselves, they are seldom taught how. Some commonly used calming techniques include: counting from one to ten, engaging in vigorous physical exercise such as aerobic dancing, meditation or conscious concentration on controlling breathing, and physically relaxing parts of your body.

An additional technique is to use "HALT" as a warning signal to slow down and to watch for stress effects. HALT stands for Hungry, Angry, Lonely, Tired. Any of these conditions makes it more difficult to handle stresses, and makes it more likely that a child will overreact to a situation in an irrational fashion. Some families have successfully used HALT as a softly spoken code word to alert the child to check his physical tension level as well as his self-talk.

Sleep has long been recognized as an effective stress management tool. Though scientists do not yet understand how, they realize that Shakespeare was right when he described "sleep that knits up the raveled sleeve of care."

Tension situations can be handled with humor. Most gifted children are able to develop a fine sense of humor quite early, and especially are able to focus on absurdities in situations. This sense of humor can be a most valuable tool for handling stress, particularly if your child can develop the ability to laugh at herself and her situations. Such humor is a clear signal that the child is able to maintain a sense of perspective, and that the stressful situation really is not awful and catastrophic. We are not talking here about cynical laughter that covers anger and disappointed idealism. Though it may reduce stress somewhat, such derisive humor is similar to blaming and implies that nothing can be done to change a bad situation.

Humor with gifted children must be handled carefully, particularly at first. They may think that you are laughing at them or ridiculing them, rather than trying to teach them to laugh at themselves. It helps if adults can demonstrate or model this humor. Sometimes you might try being melodramatic about your own situation — where it is clear that you are gently laughing at yourself. Remember that a "tragedy" pushed far enough becomes a comedy — but a comedy pushed too far becomes a tragedy.

In interpersonal situations, gifted children find humor to be useful. In addition to attracting attention for their quick wit in ways that are appreciated by their peers, they can also use humor to divert attention from stressful encounters. As one child said, "Where being smart is handy is when others try to put you down. You can turn it around and make it a joke."

The gifted child can control tense situations by expressing appreciation and understanding for others who are upset or critical of him. For a child to extend a calm offer of help or to make an empathetic statement is often so surprising to others that it defuses a potentially explosive situation. Children usually are quick to "rise to the bait" when they are being challenged or threatened. To offer to be cooperative and helpful in such a situation is quite disarming and can create the beginnings of a cooperative relationship.

Cope with stressful situations through "active ignoring." Most people think of ignoring as a passive activity; actually it is more effective as an active one. Purposely think of something other than the stressful thought or situation. Actively engage in another activity. Active ignoring works for feelings and thoughts as well as for tense situations. It is impossible to consciously think of two separate things simultaneously. Thus, by actively filling your awareness with one thought, you are actively ignoring another. Filling your awareness with a symphony can keep you from useless fretting.

Learn to question "Whose problem is it?" Much stress results from the false assumption that what the child wants is the same as what you or other adults expect from her. She may want something quite different, but the two of you may not have talked about this. It is important to check these unspoken assumptions.

The expectations of others usually cause continuous concerns for the gifted child. His expectations of himself are so often different from what others expect of him, that these mismatched expectations create tensions. When his and others' expectations are at cross-purposes and when criticism exists, it is essential that gifted children learn to define who "owns" the problem.

In their self-talk gifted children need to build in a chain of thought such as the following. "Just because they say something about me doesn't make it so. I'll decide if I think it is accurate. Then I will decide what, if anything, I want to do about it." There are three important elements in this chain of thought. First, whether criticisms about the child are accurate. The child must sort this out, particularly if it is a statement that is made about his character, beliefs or behavior. Second, deciding if he wants to do anything about it. What they say might be true, but he may choose not to do anything about it; or it might be false, but he will decide that he does need to do something. And third, the child must decide what, specifically, he wishes to do.

An example may help. If a teacher says that your child is "rude," your child will need to decide whether that is true. Then she will need to decide whether she wants to do anything about it — whether it is important to her. If it is, then she must decide *what* she wants to do. This technique will help the child learn not to assume indiscriminately the burdens, responsibilities or criticisms that others may try to give to her. We are not saying that you cannot participate in helping your child make these decisions. As in learning any other skill, she will need your guidance and patient assistance as she struggles to think through these choices.

Overall, our approach to stress management points up the importance of helping gifted children develop an awareness of their own personal priorities and values. In the final analysis they must rely on their own judgment of their adequacy as people if they are to keep life's stresses manageable. Knowledge of their own values, priorities and beliefs, combined with stress management skills, will help children have confidence in their ability to manage themselves in our world of extensive alternatives — alternatives that are more expanded due to their intellectual abilities.

The importance of stress management for gifted children and adults was corroborated in the longitudinal study by Vaillant (1977). Selected because they were rated as the best and brightest of their class at a "highly competitive college" in the Northeast (apparently Harvard), 268 men were studied through interviews and tests over a 35 year period. Though all had apparently brilliant futures ahead of them, many fell far short in their careers or their personal lives. What distinguished those who succeeded from those who did not was not the amount or type of life stresses they experienced; the lives of all contained stressful events. The difference was that the successful ones had developed strategies for coping with the stresses of life's challenges.

References

Eberle, B. *Visual Thinking: A "Scamper" Tool for Useful Imaging.* Buffalo, N.Y.: D.O.K. Publishers, 1982.

Ellis, A. and Harper, R.A. *A New Guide to Rational Living.* N.Y.: Institute for Rational Living, 1975.

Hollingworth, L.S. *Children Above 180 IQ.* N.Y.: Arno Press, 1975 (Reprint of 1942 edition).

Strang, R. Mental hygiene of gifted children. In P. Witty (Ed.), *The Gifted Child.* Lexington, Mass.: D.C. Heath, 1951.

Vaillant, G.E. *Adaptation to Life.* N.Y.: Little, Brown and Co., 1977.

Whitmore, J.R. *Giftedness, Conflict and Underachievement.* Boston: Allyn and Bacon, 1980.

Some Frequent Questions About Stress

Nightmares are particularly stressful for my child. His overactive imagination seems to continue even when he's asleep.

Many gifted children do have quite vivid dreams. If he awakens with a nightmare, first comfort him and listen to the nightmare as he describes it. Then suggest in a reassuring way that he go back to sleep and finish his dream — but this time he is to take with him into his dream whomever he would like! He can take Superman, you, or the entire U.S. Marines. Remind him that since it is *his* dream, he can finish it however he would like. He is in control, and can make it turn out any way he wants.

My problem seems just the opposite. My child seems not to have any stresses. Everything comes so easily to him.

For the most persons there is an optimum level of stress — enough to be challenging, but not so much as to be overly frustrating. Remember that persons learn to handle stress by doing so. If they are not used to meeting challenges, they often feel overwhelmed the first time they encounter situations that seem beyond their control or other major stresses. Enrichment experiences and challenging situations may help him develop coping skills and a tolerance for stressful situations. Sometimes a musical instrument will continually provide this as well as giving rewarding pleasures.

I don't think it's stressful, but my child is just overly mature. She takes matters very seriously and is quite irritated with others who don't have depth of appreciation of the implications of the issues.

This is a stressful situation indeed! Adult problems are too heavy a burden for children — even gifted ones. It is important that your child learn to balance her seriousness with humor and perspective. It is particularly important that she learn to tolerate others who see matters differently, and find dimensions within them that she can value. Otherwise she will accumulate stress and may feel that she has few, if any, persons with whom she can communicate. Encourage her to develop recreational interests so that she can learn to relax and to avoid "burn-out." Please do not confuse intellectual concern with emotional maturity.

My in-laws think that I'm being pushy because their grandchild is bored in school. They think that I've been coaching him at home, teaching him to read early, and that this is putting him under too much stress. I haven't been doing this at all; he's just taught himself to read from "Sesame Street" and "The Electric Company" on TV! How can I get them to understand?

It is often difficult to help others understand gifted children, and we hope that you will realize that you do not need to defend yourself. It may take a while to increase their awareness, along with several discussions and perhaps your supplying them with some reading material. Studies have shown that very early reading, when *self-introduced*, does not harm gifted children, and is not overly stressful. Gifted children usually enjoy these challenges. Continue to believe in yourself!

Are gifted children particularly likely to overschedule themselves? She tries to belong to every club in school, play all the sports, take every regular and optional class, and maintain a social life that would put Washington, D.C. to shame. I'm afraid she is going to burn herself out.

Particularly as they get older, gifted children do get themselves overscheduled. Although most of them thrive on it, and actively seek the stimulation it brings, their schedules can reach a point of virtual tyranny — for you, if not for them. At some point she, too, will find it frustrating, and perhaps this will provide you an opportunity to discuss the situation with her. You may be able to reassure her that all persons need private time in which to regroup and consolidate themselves, and to reflect on their experiences. In most instances there is no need for you to worry about such children causing themselves permanent physical harm — at least not if you have provided your child with an accepting atmosphere. In most children the activity level is self-regulating. That is, when they feel overstressed or tired, they will stop or slow down if they feel that it would be acceptable to do so. In younger children, though, this may not be the case, and you may have to temporarily set a limit requiring brief quiet time. In older children there is one particular problem you should perhaps be alert to — the child who frantically engages in activities as a way of proving to herself that she is worthwhile, or as a way of avoiding coming to grips with herself in an introspective way. Except for this, however, we would generally advise you primarily to try to manage your own stress from the overscheduling; see if you can find ways to enjoy watching your child's activities and accomplishments, rather than getting caught up in frantic feelings which can remove the enjoyment.

Are competitive games harmful? My gifted child seems to always want to compete with everyone.

Competitive games are emotionally and mentally stimulating, and this may be why gifted children find them so attractive. It is indeed frequent that gifted children become highly involved either with games such as chess or backgammon where a person wins or loses, or with electronic games where they test their skill against the machine. Our experience suggests that competitive games are not harmful as long as the child can demonstrate the capacity to also engage in cooperative, noncompetitive endeavors, and can see the value of cooperation with others.

"Words are, of course, the most powerful drug used by mankind."

Rudyard Kipling

"Emotion is not something shameful, subordinate, second rate; it is a supremely valid phase of humanity at its noblest and most mature."

Joshua Loth Liebman

"Regarding feelings, all of us are more children than we are anything else."

Ronald E. Fox

"By starving emotions we become humorless, rigid and stereotyped; by repressing them we become literal, reformatory and holier-than-thou; encouraged, they perfume life; discouraged, they poison it."

Joseph Collins

"Kindness in words creates confidence. Kindness in thinking creates profoundness. Kindness in giving creates love."

Lao-tzu

CHAPTER VII

COMMUNICATION OF FEELINGS

Most books and articles about gifted children focus on their intellectual prowess and on stimulating, enriching or otherwise expanding their cognitive abilities. Little has been written about emotional development. Programs in schools place intense effort on achievement in acquiring facts and knowing laws of the natural sciences. The areas of communication, feelings, interpersonal relations and social sciences receive only the smallest attention, perhaps within a teaching module called *Affective Education,* despite repeated studies demonstrating that emotions have a major effect on achievement and IQ test scores (Sattler, 1982).

We feel the emphasis is out of balance, although it is understandable. The common view in our country is that education should be aimed toward measurable achievement and preparation for vocations, and that values, beliefs, and personal and emotional development should be taught at home. It may not be too harsh even to say that most school systems view feelings as obstructive nuisances to be managed so that they do not interfere with the main business of learning. Our observations suggest an even more tragic pattern: parents, too, may avoid, ignore, or discredit their children's feelings to keep those feelings from interfering with family business.

Communication of feelings is the most important psychological lifeline available to any person, especially to a child. While a negative attitude toward feelings can be harmful to any child, the gifted child may be especially vulnerable because so much of the activity surrounding him, so much of the attention focused on him, prizes only achievement and emphasizes only cognitive skills. It is particularly important that we develop methods for insuring safe, non-threatening, and valid expression of feelings for the gifted child. Several studies have pointed out that children who live in emotionally deprived situations with little expression of interpersonal caring show a decline in their measured intelligence (Marland, 1972).

Because gifted children have extraordinary abilities for abstract and divergent thinking, developed at a relatively early age, their ways of thinking are different from others. Their curiosity, advanced verbal abilities and high skill level may make them appear "better" than others. People around them usually react strongly to these differences, often negatively — with anger, sarcasm and criticism. Because his attempts to express his perceptions and interpretations are so often frustrated, the gifted child may prefer to keep his feelings and opinions to himself. He may come to feel that thinking or feeling differently is neither accepted nor allowed, or that there is something fundamentally wrong with him as a person.

This frustration is heightened by the gifted child's awareness that his sensitivity, intensity and curiosity are his strengths, yet they are the source of his problems with others. As one child noted, "We tend to be much more sensitive than other people. Multiple meanings, innuendos and self-consciousness plague us. Intensive self-analysis, self-criticism, and the inability to recognize that we have limits make us despondent. In fact, most times our self-searching leaves us more discombobbled than we were at the outset" (American Association for Gifted Children, 1978).

Killer Statements

The strong feelings and reactions of others, particularly adults, can interfere with the honest communication that should be natural to these sensitive youngsters. Siblings, peers, teachers and even parents often react to gifted children as if they are undisciplined, bossy and rude, and that they need to be "put in their place" or "taken down a peg." As most gifted children will confirm, many of the remarks made to them are unfair — "low blows" from which it is difficult to recover. We have come to call such statements "Killer Statements," since they have the potential of bringing honest communication to a standstill. We have summarized some of the more common Killer Statements in Table 9.

All of these statements tell the child in one way or another that he is not acceptable as he is, that he is fundamentally inadequate or incompetent. Repeated exposure to such evaluative comments can stunt the gifted child's emotional growth and set the stage for emotional withdrawal, insecurity, poor self-concept and a deep distrust of interpersonal relationships.

Although few of us can be certain that we will *never* use one, such statements should be recognized as dangerous weapons and avoided as thoroughly as possible. Even persons with good intentions may subtly, thoughtlessly or unconsciously use variations of these insensitive statements, thereby impairing trust and the honest expression of real feelings. When a Killer Statement does slip out because of frustration, impatience or anger, it is important to explain your underlying feelings and to apologize. The expression of regret or apology by an adult, even after the passage of time, is a model for open communication, respect, trust and acceptance of feelings.

It is indeed fortunate that children are as resilient as they are. Perhaps it is the extra mental adroitness of gifted children that

Table 9

"Killer Statements"
(Guaranteed to inhibit communication and motivation)

- Stop living in an ivory tower! Be like the rest of the world!
- We don't have time for that now! Don't bother me!
- That's a stupid idea; you know that's impossible!
- With your memory, I don't believe you really forgot! I think you didn't want to do it!
- If I had wanted it done any other way, I would have said so!
- For someone so smart you sure can act dumb!
- You don't have any common sense at all! Why can't you be like your brother?
- I just don't know what's gotten into you these days! You're so out of it!
- Where were you when I was explaining all that – asleep?
- You're always thinking of yourself – never about anyone else!
- I've had it with you! Just get out of here with your silly ideas!
- You don't really believe that! You've just let yourself be influenced by those strange friends of yours.
- That idea isn't new, you know. It was discovered years ago!
- You're not ready for that. It just won't work, and would just be a waste of time!
- I don't care what you think – do it like I said!
- You're just going through a stage – you'll outgrow it.
- Stop being so childish and immature! When you grow up you'll know how you should feel about these things!
- You have no right to feel that way! Your attitude is just wrong!
- Just straighten up and shake it off – you're just feeling sorry for yourself!
- I don't want any of your moodiness today – you'll spoil the day for everyone else.
- What makes you think you're so special? – Everybody's got problems! You want to hear problems? Let me tell you. . . !
- You'll do it because I said so!

allows so many of them to survive as well as they do. Because Killer Statements are used against them routinely, and because of society's fundamental ambivalence about them, gifted children — far from being better off than others — actually need extra emotional support or "strokes." The higher the range of giftedness and the farther the child from the norm, the more vital is this truth. It is important to teach the child what he can do to get these strokes, and to provide as much emotional support as possible.

One Person Can Be a Key

In our experience the number of people from whom a child receives emotional support is less important than the intensity of the support he gets from any one person. If the child has even one person who conveys genuine belief in him and with whom he communicates freely and feels accepted, he will be able to overcome much negativity. Having just one real haven allows the child to withstand many unjust situations and many hostile responses from others. The key person could be you, a special friend, a mentor, a sibling, a teacher — anyone. What is essential is that your child have at least one person who validates him as a person, one person who can assure him that what he feels and believes in is reasonable and worthwhile, that he has value.

How to Foster Communication

Once you are aware of the dangers of Killer Statements, you can take positive steps to foster or to improve communication between you and your gifted child.

You cannot force communication with someone. As one colleague says, "It's like trying to push a rope; the harder you push, the more it squiggles away from you." There are things you can do, though, to create an atmosphere that will foster communication. These primarily involve recognizing that feelings should not be denied or avoided; they are useful aspects of human behavior.

To establish communication, recognize and express authentic feelings yourself. Albert Schweitzer once said, "In teaching children, demonstrating is not just the best way; often it is the only way." Disclosing your own feelings and values will promote a similar expression by others. Self-disclosure begets self-disclosure. Sharing your feelings not only provides information the other person may need, but establishes a level of trust that encourages the other person to reciprocate.

If you share not only the positive feelings, but some of the more poignant ones, such as fear, hurt or embarrassment, you allow others to care for you, to be nurturing. Our experience has been that most children will not take advantage of these delicate feelings when they are expressed with genuine trust. It is well to avoid "dumping" feelings, however. Carelessly throwing out your feelings without regard for the effect they might have on others does not help to create trust and may work against communication.

Remember that trying to deny or cover up your own feelings tends to breed distrust, alienation and lack of confidence in a relationship. What others are willing to communicate to you depends on how they see you and how safe they believe they will be after revealing their emotions. If they see that you are not comfortable with your own feelings, they will be unlikely to trust you with theirs.

Every communication has an emotional component, and the content of what is communicated is affected by it. The emotional aspect of communication may be carried by your tone of voice through inflection, volume, etc. or by body language through your posture and gestures. The same content can be expressed in varied emotions, and will be received differently by others as a result. You can become more aware of this through a simple exercise — recite the letters of the alphabet first in a happy way, then with sadness, and finally angrily. The content is the same; your inflection and tone are not.

Be aware of the emotions you convey to others through these means. Many people are unaware that they generally sound angry or disinterested in others. It can be revealing for you to put yourself on mental "instant replay" to hear the emotional messages you are communicating. Ask your children and others. Perhaps even tape record or video-tape yourself to discover how you sound or what body messages you are sending, and whether they are the ones you wish to send. Your children might enjoy doing these exercises themselves, and it could help them in their interactions with their friends.

Avoid sending your children self-contradictory messages. The words say one thing: the voice tone and body language say another! For example, a mother might say, "I really would like to hear about your day," in such a bored tone of voice that the boredom overrides the content. When the emotional message contradicts the words, a confused or even fearful child may result. Usually, the child believes the tone of voice. Someone needs to explain to the child how such double messages occur, and whoever is sending double messages needs to check himself to see which message he really intends.

Labels for feelings are helpful, and gifted children can learn accurate labels for their feelings quite early in life. They need this information to sort out messages that are being communicated and to establish further emotional development. They also need to learn that feelings tend to be automatic, like internal reflexes, and cannot usually be directly or immediately controlled. Feelings themselves may be more or less strong, more or less comfortable — but they are not "right" or "wrong." It is the behaviors that result from these feelings that can be controlled, shaped and judged. For preschool children we have found *T.A. for Tots* (Freed, 1974) to be an excellent resource regarding feeling labels, along with *T.A. for Kids* (Freed, 1976) for older ones.

Accept the Feelings

Accepting a child's feelings and thoughts does *not* mean you agree with them. Feelings belong only to the person who has them. As one parent said, "There are very few things that a person truly owns in this world, but feelings — those are yours and no one else's." It is not helpful to tell a child that he "shouldn't" feel a particular way or "has no right" to a certain feeling. You can no more order an emotion out of existence than you can order Niagara Falls to stop falling.

Feelings are so reflexive that they are not logical. Gifted children, particularly those who are "left-brained" and prefer a world of logic and order, may have difficulty handling feelings. They need reassurance that feelings need not be logical, that they are not orderly, and that a person may have several different feelings about a given person or situation all at the same time.

Statements of understanding should always precede statements of advice, action or instruction, particularly if feelings are running high. If you can put into words some understanding of how a person might feel in the situation being dealt with, some of the feelings may be defused. Until a child's feelings are dealt with, it is very hard for him to be "reasonable" or empathetic with the feelings of others. Just by communicating to your child that you understand his situation and what bothers him about it, you support the child's self-concept. This is particularly important when you must discipline or correct him. You might think of this as the "sandwich technique." Sandwich your complaint between a positive statement of understanding and a closing comment of encouragement or appreciation. Such a subtlety of approach is not lost on a gifted child.

Feelings should not become an area for a power struggle. Try to avoid a mental set that demands a "win," or presents you as the "old pro" able to hand out ready-made solutions to a problem that clearly involves a lot of the child's feelings. Such a competitive or dogmatically authoritative approach is discouraging to the child. It tells him that you know better than he does what is good for him — that you believe you know his feelings even better than he does. Instead, help him realize he can deal with his own feelings and generally can arrive at his own solutions.

Let your child know that you do not expect him to be perfect or to have the solution to his own and everyone else's problems — particularly their personal problems. It helps if you let it be known that you are not perfect, that you sometimes fail to live up to your ideals or values, and that you do not have all the answers. You change as you learn and grow in life, and if you let him know it, he will find it easier to reveal his own inconsistencies and emotional complexities. Sadly, too many cases have illustrated to us that believing in one's potential for perfection can be paralyzing.

When you express confidence in your child and appreciation for his past communications, you encourage him to continue to communicate his feelings and beliefs. He needs to have confidence that his views are valued and that if he reveals to you what is really on his mind, you will not use it to punish him. He must believe that sharing his thoughts and feelings will work for him rather than against him.

Be careful about making promises, especially about promising to keep a secret before you know what it is. In particular, your children need to be able to trust that you will not violate confidences.

All children have certain areas of life in which feelings are as sacred to them as the crown jewels are to England. Although it may seem foolish and illogical to you, you must respect these areas with special sensitivity. Your children deserve that you be particularly gentle with these feelings, and that you not make fun of them or thoughtlessly share them with others. As children reach adolescence, their emotional oversensitivity will probably increase. Then you will need to be especially careful not to indicate that their feelings are not "real," or that they have no right to their feelings, are "dumb" for having such feelings, or that they are in a childish stage they will outgrow. The delicacy of such feelings has prompted helpful books such as *Why Am I Afraid to Tell You Who I Am* (Powell, 1969).

Handling feelings with diplomacy can be challenging for parents because gifted children sometimes seem to have an overflow of feelings and to handle them clumsily. As one parent said, "The main trouble with kids is that they're so childish and immature in their feelings!" Of course they are! That is part of being a child, gifted or not. Learning to communicate and handle feelings is not an easy task and children are seldom skilled at it because they have not lived long enough to accumulate the experience and practice.

Some gifted children, teenagers in particular, will act as though they have no feelings and they do not care in the least what others think of them. If you encounter this in your child, please remember that it is almost certainly a facade — everyone has feelings. Remember the milk industry slogan, "You never outgrow your need for milk." This is particularly true of the milk of human kindness, support, and emotional stroking. Usually when kids deny that they have feelings, it means that the feelings are too sensitive to be dealt with or that they are afraid that their feelings would not be accepted or appreciated if they were expressed.

Listening Is Communicating

Sometimes it is possible to become aware of underlying feelings by listening with an "extra ear," particularly when gifted children express worry or concern about social issues or abstract ideas. For example, "When people die, do they ever come back to life?" may be a way of asking "What will happen when *I* die?" You may also notice a great curiosity or concern about teenagers pregnancy or the rights of the underprivileged, when your child is actually asking for reassurance about a personal concern of his within the family.

We cannot emphasize too strongly the importance of listening. When a parent really listens, he conveys that the child's ideas, feelings and values are worthwhile — worth listening to. This is especially important and encouraging for the gifted child whose ideas may be out of step with his peers. Often, children just want you to listen, and nothing more. In lending an ear, you give confirmation that they are important. They do not want comments, opinions or evaluations — just an accepting ear and a chance to share their feelings, whether of frustration or joy. You may find that you need to ask your child, "Do you want me to give an opinion, or do you just want me to listen and share the feeling?"

Specific Suggestions to Enhance Communication

It helps to have in your repertoire some skills to make your listening a more active endeavor. As you listen to a conversation, try to *respond by reflecting the feelings* that seem to be underlying what your child is saying. This can be done without being elaborate, and often the more succinct, the better. Sometimes just a syllable, an "Mmmm," or the repetition of a key word with emphasis is enough. This way the only addition you make to the conversation is your interest. Active listening can be nurturing. It can serve as a mirror in which your child can see his feelings and attitudes reflected so he may be able to control his behavior more objectively.

Be alert to barriers to communication such as T.V., newspapers or pastimes. Sometimes focusing on these outside concerns may be merely a habit the family has drifted into. Other times, it is an intentional means to avoid communication. In any case, varying the routine is helpful. Situations which bind people tightly into old roles and old assumptions rarely allow personalities to move freely along creative courses.

The *"special time"* technique decidedly fosters communication, regardless of the child's age. Parents should attempt to insure that each child has a few minutes of uninterrupted special time each day in which the child has your complete attention. If you have several children, you can set the kitchen timer for five minutes to designate that period when you will not accept interruptions from the others — unless someone is bleeding! When your child sees you refuse to take a phone call because "it's my special time with Suzy," it makes an impression. She realizes that you view time with her as important. What you talk about or what you do during this time is less important than the fact that the time belongs to the child, no matter what.

Parents can come up with creative variations for special time. One parent can drive a child to school, or take a child out alone to breakfast at a restaurant. Bike rides or walks to the store can be arranged. Playing cards is another way to share time together. Remember, the frequency of the special times counts more than the duration. Five special times of ten minutes each are more effective than one special period of fifty minutes.

Share an activity that is important to your child or to you. Many of us think of going to watch the child play ball but do not consider that the child might enjoy joining us in one of our activities.

You might take a child into the office on a weekend for special time to run off a report on the computer and then staple the extra copies. The two of you can undertake such a project jointly. Just as actively participating in your child's work or interests shows that you care about what is important to him, including him in your activities shows that you want his involvement and view him as a person worth including.

"Running away from home" together for a day or a weekend can give you a lot of special time with your child. You can also go camping. Or take the child along on a business trip. An amazing amount of communication and development of trust can occur in a three hour car trip to another city. You can still have your meeting or your speaking engagement, but add a museum trip or a visit to the zoo before you return home. All of these activities prompt you and your child to break out of the ritual roles you may have drifted into, and promote new ways of relating to each other.

A special place can be as important as a special time. Feelings of being safe and understood can be associated with a room, a particular sofa or other special place. Snuggling on the over-stuffed grandfather's chair or under the backyard trees can prompt intimate communication and the expectation that the child will be cuddled and cared for. Sometimes just leading your child to this haven will be enough reassurance for him to respond.

When Problems Occur

Despite your best efforts, communication problems can develop. Strong feelings arise and there may be an emotional confrontation. You are wondering what you can do. We do not pretend to have the answer to all problems, but perhaps we can offer some helpful hints.

First, remember that feelings are transient. The crisis will pass. It also helps if you have communicated this to your children, who may be feeling that whatever emotion is peaking at this moment will go on at this level forever. It is helpful if both parties know that emotional peaks are not going to be maintained indefinitely. On the other hand, be aware that strong feelings do not go away just because you order them to! Lecturing a child about how he "should" feel usually provokes further irritation. Accept his feelings with reasonable sympathy, even if they are directed against you.

Recognize, perhaps aloud, that sorting out solutions to emotional dilemmas or confrontations is difficult, and that each person must work it out largely on his own. Do not spoon-feed *your* solutions to the child and expect them to work. He will need to discover his own solutions, though you may be able to assist him in that discovery. Unless he really believes an answer to a problem, he is not likely to make it part of his thinking. Your ability to let him think through his painful situation is an expression of trust and will create confidence in your child.

Although you may not want to actively search for communication problems within your family, you need not avoid coming to grips with difficult feelings. In fact, if you do not allow negative feelings to be communicated, they build up and leak out, explode, or are acted out in some way that usually is not only destructive, but also self-defeating. Sometimes these stored up negative feelings are expressed in an indirect fashion — especially if there is no complaint department within the family. For example, the child of a teacher may choose to get low grades to punish his father for trying to control him rather than risking an irate reaction if he expresses his resentment of his father's domination. Another child may express inappropriate rage at his flat bicycle tire; this is safer than showing the fury he feels toward his overly protective mother who makes him feel incompetent.

In summary, though feelings are often overlooked, they are extremely important in working with gifted children. If you want to know someone's feelings, you must offer a posture that is receptive, without intruding or forcing your way in. You cannot require people to share their feelings with you — but you can make it both easy and rewarding.

References

American Association for Gifted Gildren. *On Being Gifted.* New York: Walker and Co., 1978.

Freed, A.M. *T.A. for Tots.* Sacramento: Jalmar Press, Inc., 1974.

Freed, A.M. *T.A. for Kids.* Sacramento: Jalmar Press, Inc., 1976.

Marland, S. *Education of the Gifted and Talented,* U.S. Commission of Education, 92nd Cong., 2nd Session, Washington, D.C.: USCPO, 1972.

Powell, J. *Why Am I Afraid to Tell You Who I Am?* Niles, Ill.: Argus Communications, 1969.

Sattler, J.M. *Assessment of Children's Intelligence and Special Abilities.* Boston: Allyn and Bacon, 1982.

Some Frequent Questions
About Communication of Feelings

How can I make my child communicate with me? He has totally shut me out!

You can't *force* your child to communicate with you if he does not want to — at least not honestly. Change your thinking to "How can I *encourage* my child to *want* to communicate with me?" You must not expect instant total communication. A relationship takes time to develop. The more you try to force your child to open up, the more he will be like a turtle who withdraws into his shell when people pick at him.

Don't parents have a right to their feelings also? It seems like everything you have said focuses on helping the child.

Of course parents have a right to their feelings. If there is anything in this life that people have a right to, it is their feelings. Most of what has been covered in this section can apply to relating with any other person, adult or child. We assume, though, that most parents can modify their behavior and have better control over their emotions than do children. Our experience suggests that when parents begin to express understanding of their children's feelings, the children then begin to model after their parents and show more empathy and appreciation of their parents' feelings.

Don't we run a risk of having a child who is oversensitive and who embarrasses himself and us by expressing even the smallest private feelings?

Children need to learn what their feelings are, and how and where to express them. They can only do this with practice and with good role models. The more comfortable they are with their feelings, the less likely children are to express them inappropriately. Rather than being oversensitive, the child is more likely to be more fully aware and in control of himself, his values, and his feelings, and because of this, to have greater empathy with others.

How much am I hurting my child with my killer statements? As hard as I try, sometimes these statements just burst out!

Fortunately children, and particularly gifted children, are very resilient and forgiving. If your killer statements are infrequent, and if there is a complaint department in the family, a safe moment where support is given, then these children will usually tell you when they are hurting — if you are able to listen and will allow them to tell you. An apology and genuine attempts to improve can be very nurturing.

I do express my feelings and try to receive my child's feelings, but he still seems withdrawn.

It often helps to examine *what* feelings you are communicating through your words, tone of voice and body language. Perhaps in your attempts to achieve openness you may have also increased the number of negatives you express. Without being hypocritical, if you try to convey more positives than negatives, you may supply the courage and hope which can be the fuel for enthusiasm and pride. You may even want to set your goal to make 90% of your expressions positive! That would be an ideal, and we hope you try for it.

"I reckon there's as much human nature in some folks as there is in others, if not more."

Edward Noyes Westcott

"No man is an island entire of itself; every man is a piece of a continent, part of the main."

John Donne

"Let's go hand in hand, not one before another."

William Shakespeare

"If a man does not keep pace with his companions, perhaps it is because he hears a different drummer."

Henry David Thoreau

"I don't want to be a genius . . . I have problems enough just trying to be a man."

Albert Camus

CHAPTER VIII

PEER RELATIONSHIPS

We know gifted children voted the "most popular," the "most likely to succeed," and the "most preppy." Without looking for problems, we also know many who have a hard time fitting in. In the typical neighborhood or classroom the number of highly intelligent children may be limited, and thus there may be few available associates who appreciate the same things as they.

When kindergarten starts, so may peer problems. This could be due to lack of experience in dealing with others, or to the sudden frustration brought on by their encounters with others who do not share interests, attitudes or behaviors.

Even though they usually learn to cope in some fashion or another, gifted children continually must adapt themselves to a norm that is quite different from the way they have come to know themselves. Often they dislike the term "gifted" because they feel it alienates them from their friends, although at the same time they often admit that they find it pleasing and even flattering. The desire to conform and fit in comes into conflict with the expression of unique talents. As one student said, "To put it simply, my friends were an obstacle in my academic progress. I was so hung up in conforming to what they expected of me that I did not take my school work seriously as I should have." Another student took a more positive view of peer pressure as a task "one must overcome, and . . . you should

regard it simply as such." (American Association for Gifted
Children, 1978).

Are Peers Really Equal?

With gifted children, perhaps more than with any other group,
it is important first to look at who are their peers, and to help
the gifted child understand what a peer is. Peers are persons of
equal rank or standing. But who is "equal" to a gifted child? In
what activities and what situations? The child's peer in soccer
may not be that child's peer in chess or in mathematics. At any
time gifted children will have various peers, depending on what
intellectual, emotional, physical or situational relationships they
are involved in. The concept of peer relations is not a simple one,
and we cannot assume that children are equals just because they
are the same age.

Inclusion, Control and Affection

In relating to peers, at least one of three major issues is usually involved — inclusion/exclusion, control, affection (Schutz,
1958.) Peer-related behavior can be understood more easily
when these three dimensions are considered. At first glance,
these three may appear similar, but they are not. The issue of
whether one is included or excluded is the most basic dimension
— whether one is part of the in-group or the out-group, or altogether without a group. After this has been decided, the next
issue is who is in control of any group — who is a leader, who is
a follower, who is a facilitator, etc. Usually it is only after these
two issues are settled that the third one arises — whether others
in the group feel lasting affection for you. Typically you feel
affection only for those whom you can count on, and whose
behavior is predictable. To depend on someone, you must first

know whether you are included in the group, and then you must know your own and the other's role in that group.

Feeling included, respected and cared about by friends is important to all children. Peer acceptance is necessary to develop a healthy self-image and a continuing sense of worth. To be accepted by others implies that you have met at least a moderate number of their expectations — that you have conformed sufficiently to allow at least some communication, understanding and respect.

Places to Practice and Compare

Interacting with others of the same age or ability level is a major source of learning where children practice social and behavioral skills, and get feedback about themselves. In this socialization process they compare themselves with others along various dimensions — size, physical skills, social skills, mental skills. They continually consider the question, "How do I compare with others?" and the answers influence their developing self-concept. Entering school, where there is a new set of expectations, particularly fosters comparisons, and later the insecurities of adolescence make comparisons even more intense.

Unfortunately, however, many children's comparisons are inappropriate since children may be square pegs attempting to fit themselves into round hole groups. The leveling process involved in peer socialization may shave off their corners. Unless someone has pointed it out to them, gifted children are usually unaware that they will need several different peer groups and that they may be comparing themselves to the wrong peer group for a particular aspect of themselves at a particular time. Younger gifted children are especially likely to think that others can do all the things they can do, that others should enjoy all the various things they enjoy, and that others view the world in the same way as they. Thus, their attempts to communicate with their age peers and to fit in often results in confusion, lack of appreciation and hurt feelings. The following interaction between a six year old gifted child and his seven year old next door neighbor, a child of only above average ability, provides an example. He began telling her some riddles — his current obsession.

> HE: What is Wild Bill Hiccup's favorite color?
> SHE: I don't know.
> HE: Burple. (laughs)
> SHE: (Stares at him, not laughing)

(He tries others; her reaction is the same. Finally, wanting to get in on the action, she tries one.)

> SHE: What does the little girl say when her mother asks what her favorite colors are?
> HE: (Thinking hard for the joke answer — finally gives up) What?
> SHE: Red, yellow and piple.
> HE: (Stares uncomprehendingly while she laughs) What's funny about that?
> SHE: The little girl can't say purple, so she says piple instead.
> HE: (The model of tact) That's dumb!
> SHE: (Wounded) It is not!
> HE: What did one candle say to the other candle?
> SHE: What?
> HE: Are you going out tonight? HA HA HA!
> SHE: (Just looks at him) What did one mitten say to the other mitten?
> HE: (Thinks — again gives up) What?
> SHE: Hi, mitten.

HE: (Frustrated beyond endurance) Mary, NOT A SINGLE ONE OF YOUR RIDDLES IS EVEN FUNNY A BIT!

SHE: Well, neither are yours!

How Much Should He Fit In?

Many parents and other adults may have the inappropriate expectation that children of the same age should fit with each other in school or out. This particularly occurs if the parents have not yet come to appreciate the unusual nature of their child's particular abilities, temperament, interest and stage of development. Most parents want their child to be normal and to fit in. In our society a premium is placed on sociability. Regardless of how you feel about a person, you are expected to get along with him. Parents and other adults may put substantial pressure on their child, conveying the message that conformity is all important — more important than the inner drives of the child toward discovery and creativity. Parents and teachers of gifted children want them to be happy and accepted by other kids. Even now, we ourselves may still ache as we remember moments when we felt left out, and we can recall the euphoria of feeling "popular." It is such memories that may prompt us to be concerned about the mental well-being of a gifted child who has only a few friends and is not popular.

Because gifted children have a lot to give, they experience a wide range of adjustments, challenges, and joys with many other children. What *we* would consider satisfactory peer relationships may be quite different from what gifted children themselves feel. We have found that some gifted children, particularly ones who are exceptionally gifted, need only a few friends. Sometimes their peer needs seem to be mostly satisfied by just one special friend, typically in a relationship that is quite intense.

Such gifted children often have little interest in being "popular," particularly if this means spending time in relationships that are superficial. They would rather select fewer friends, preferring relationships with enough meaning and depth to satisfy their need to relate and to be accepted. For them, and for you, it is important to remember that having a few friends because you only *want* a few, is very different from having few friends because you do not know how to obtain or keep friends, or because you are afraid of being rejected or of feeling unacceptable.

Even so, most gifted children would like very much to have a wide range of meaningful relationships, and many of them do want to be popular even at the sacrifice of some of their own interests. These children usually try to fit into several peer groups at the same time. Parents may have to do a lot of extra driving, and may be surprised by the variety of groups and the age span of friends. Mixed-age groups, such as are found at hobby shops, are typical for gifted children.

Special Friendships

Whether your child has few friends or many friends, we believe that most gifted children need to have one most valued relationship. This special friend provides a haven where the child's uniqueness is appreciated, a haven which helps the child tolerate the pressures, slights and insults he may receive from others. The conversations with this special friend allow the child to develop a different perspective on the situations with which he will be confronted, to give and receive affection, and to receive validation of his own worth.

Although such special friends are important to the gifted child because of her intensity and emotional sensitivity, we do feel that other peer relationships are also desirable. We would like for you to encourage your child to develop a network of relationships, though you will need to understand that it may be difficult for her. Such a network helps her develop an appreciation of the value and contributions of others who are less bright than she. One of the most significant tasks facing these children is that of adjusting to the varying expectations of different individuals and groups.

Whan I Was Labeled 'Gifted,' Then . . .

The *public* identification of a child as gifted sometimes causes peer relationship problems. When a child is labeled gifted, his peers are likely to automatically assume that they are "non-gifted," and thus that they have been unfairly left out in some fashion. One child noted "I was told too many times in the wrong company that I was smart. The wrong company . . . is my peers. . . . I hated being at the head of the class, Naturally, my peers hated me too. But the self-hatred was more intense." (American Association for Gifted Children, 1978).

Though many teachers do attempt to foster support and acceptance of gifted children, we have heard enough horror stories to convince us that there are teachers who apparently resent them, and who purposely ridicule them. Seemingly, they go out of their way to make life difficult for gifted children and to make them less acceptable to their peers. One teenager offered the following description.

> "I've fortunately outgrown the bullies-in-the-schoolyard stage, not that I didn't have my share . . . of problems with them as a child. With age and maturity come newer bullies, infinitely more cunning and resourceful; I'm referring to those teachers who assume that I can handle any amount of homework they choose to give me at any given time. The trouble with these bullies is

that you can't run to teacher for help with them.
Perhaps you could run to the schoolyard?"
(American Association for Gifted Children,
1978).

When a gifted child is a high achiever, his accomplishments serve to point out the inadequacies of those who aren't achieving as highly. Even though high academic performance generally assures approval by adults, it is often threatening to peers. It is critical that parents *and* children understand this, and realize that children may face a long-term struggle between achievement and acceptance. Parents and teachers must avoid holding up a gifted child's achievement as an example to his peers, or as a way of "shaming" other children into achieving. We know of an unfortunate instance, for example, where a fourth grade teacher brought a gifted second grade student to read aloud to her class "to show them how it *should* be done." You can perhaps guess whose pants were run up the flagpole that day during recess.

In some special schools or programs for gifted children it is possible to congregate a group of gifted children, thus reducing some of the inherent peer problems. Although this approach is indeed helpful, we must point out that exceptionally gifted children may still not fit it. The range of abilities among gifted children is truly great. Persons in the top one percent of mental ability differ from each other more than persons in the four percentiles just below them. Additionally, as we have noted previously, there are several types of giftedness. Thus a gifted child may have difficulty relating to other gifted children, even though the likelihood of peer problems is reduced.

Leadership Or Bossiness?

Many gifted children have another characteristic that can lead to peer difficulties — they like to organize things and people, usually in complicated ways. Often this organization is not appreciated by peers who may feel they are being bossed, reformed or controlled. These other children may not even comprehend the concepts or language.

Gifted children can make their ability to analyze situations work for them on the issue of control. They can be taught the difference between leadership and bossiness. Effective leaders are ahead of their followers, but not so far ahead as to be out of sight. They are good listeners because they must know what others are thinking. A series of discussions about leaders and leadership, and how good management skills differ from dictatorship can help your child with many group situations.

Developing Leadership Skills

Implicit in your discussions will be developing an appreciation for the feelings of those who are following, along with instances where your child, himself, was a follower — or could have been a follower. We have found that it is particularly valuable for gifted children to *offer to help* rather than to take charge. You can help your child learn when and how to be a good follower, how to ask for help, how to help others feel important and valued, and how to improve the functioning of a group without being the group leader. They can learn to become "enablers," delegating and assisting rather than commanding, while maintaining a sense of control.

Empathy and understanding of other's viewpoints are skills that need to be nurtured. Two techniques seem particularly helpful, and gifted children usually enjoy them. These are *anticipation through fantasy* and *role-playing.*

Your child's advanced mental abilities will allow him to think through complex situations and to learn to anticipate consequences. This ability to anticipate does not just happen, however. Even a gifted child usually needs to be taught, or helped to refine his approach. This mental role play would include a series of questions like "What do you think would happen if you . . . ?" "And then what might happen?" "What do you suppose he (they) would do (think, feel, etc.) then?" "How could you respond to that?" "What else might you try?"

Follow the Socratic approach; teach by asking questions, and avoid giving answers, opinions or editorial comments. This approach shows the child that you believe she can be responsible for herself and lets her mentally experience a new situation before actually being involved, thus allowing her to consider approaches and strategies ahead of time. You can demonstrate your caring by recognizing and putting into words her peer relation problems or feelings of isolation. It is important that the child feel that her problems are understood and are significant to others. But do not try to give a quick solution — just help her think through possible alternatives. By raising questions, you can put a different light on the situation. For example, "What other things might you do besides putting her in such a win-lose position?" This can stimulate positive behaviors while preserving her ability to choose her own alternatives.

A variation of this is role-playing, to help your child understand how the other person feels and thinks. Have your child assume the role and behaviors of the other person, while you play your child's part. Gifted children usually find this approach both enjoyable and enlightening, particularly if you make your acting melodramatic to highlight your points — but with good humor. You may wish to role-play a situation several times — trying different approaches to see what would happen. Or you might switch parts.

Another way to facilitate peer relationships is to arrange for children to participate in a project in pairs. This allows an emotional bond to develop between the children. Sharing an activity is one of the best ways to create mutual respect, and has emotional advantages even if the project is something that could be done individually. It is valuable in this context for the parents to remember that the world inside the gifted child's mind may be more important to him than the social world of his peers. He may get so wrapped up in his own thoughts and actions that he ignores others. You can help him understand why this may turn others off and be self-defeating.

Gifted Teenagers

In teenage years, conformity and peer relations take on an added importance, and it is during this time that many gifted children choose to submerge their talents and sacrifice their achievements in favor of belonging. Girls in particular may decide that "It's not too smart to be too smart." Gifted teenagers are painfully aware that their peers operate on the basis of sterotypes about persons of high intelligence:

> "Intelligent people don't party, drink or date. They are the ones that stay home and work the calculus problems so that everyone can copy their homework in the morning."

> "Some people don't think I could ever be interested in their more mundane things like parties and girls."

> "Some people assume I'm conceited and untouchable, or impossible to get along with. They've heard of me but they don't know me in person; they've read the reviews and think they've read the book." (American Association for Gifted Children, 1978).

156

The gifted teenager, then, may often feel caught between strong feelings. Her desire to belong, her need for exploration, her curiosity, and her divergent, flexible, open-minded thinking may lead her to temporarily establish relationships with peers the parents feel are not particularly desirable companions. You may be able to help her think through what she is hoping to obtain or learn from these relationships, and what costs accompany having undesirable friends. Nevertheless, she may decide that it is more important for her to continue those particular friendships. If so, you will probably not be successful in trying to select or limit her friendships, and will need to recall from the chapter on Discipline that it is not helpful to set limits that you cannot enforce. You may have to tolerate your own discomfort about your child's associations within the confines of whatever appropriate limits you can and do enforce.

Perhaps the best single help you can be to your child in the area of peer relations is through providing a good model. After all, peer relationships do not end with childhood; the joys and problems continue throughout life. The examples and the understanding you provide through your own behavior will be far more important than anything you could say, although your communications with your child will add depth and clarity to the examples you provide.

References

American Association of Gifted Children. *On Being Gifted.* New York: Walker and Co., 1978.

Schutz, W.C. *FIRO-B: A Three Dimensional Theory of Interpersonal Behavior.* N.Y.: Rinehart & Co., 1958.

Some Frequent Questions About Peer Relationships

What do I say when my child says he feels alone and friendless?

First, accept his statement as really indicating how he feels right now, even though you may "know" that he has several friends. Gently ask him what he thinks are the reasons he is unaccepted. Has he always been unaccepted? Has anyone ever liked him? What was he doing then that helped others to like him? What does he think that he could be doing, perhaps without knowing it, that turns others off?

My child gets so impatient with other kids. How can I help her be more tolerant?

It helps if the child can realize that others are usually not acting out of malice. Most others are genuinely groping to find their way through life, and often act out of their own sense of frustration or lack of knowledge. It sometimes helps to raise questions about the value of human life. One patient did this successfully by talking about Darwin's theory of evolution via survival, and Hitler's holocaust extermination of the Jews and of mentally "unfit" persons. His gifted child was horrified at the notion that this was "survival of the fittest." The parent then raised questions about tolerance in present day society, and whether less gifted persons had value and deserved patience and respect. There are many other important human characteristics that are valuable besides intelligence or talent!

My child seems so cynical. How do I handle that?

Most cynicism is a cover for the idealism that is underneath. Try to respond to that frustrated, but yearning, idealism. It often helps if the child can develop a sense of humor about himself and the world.

My gifted teenager has suddenly begun to hang around with some really dumb friends. Won't this handicap his mental growth?

Probably not, even though his outward appearance might suggest otherwise. It is likely that his need to belong is out-weighing his need to achieve publicly, at least for now. This will pass as he learns to combine his peer needs with the other aspects of his life. Gifted children continue to absorb information even though they do not appear to be, and in most situations giftedness is not something that will atrophy or waste away if it is not stimulated to the maximum — at least not beyond the age of ten or twelve. Since relations with others will continue to be an important part of his life and he will continually have to make choices about his friends, use this opportunity to help him explore and develop confidence in his ability to choose and keep friends.

My child has an imaginary playmate. Is this something to worry about? Will he give this up as he makes more friends?

Gifted children seem particularly likely to develop imaginary playmates, and often require their parents to go to extemes to accommodate them. As long as your child is able to give and take feelings with you and with most others, an imaginary play-mate is nothing to worry about. Usually "Harvey" disappears when a child enters school or when a child establishes a variety of friendships. Enjoy your child's creativity and flair for the dramatic, and please do not ridicule him for having an imaginary peer!

But it's my child's nature to be a loner. He's happier just entertaining himself. Isn't it enough to be busy and content with what he's doing?

Temperamentally, some gifted children are more likely to be loners. But there is a big difference between being alone because you want to be and being a loner because you lack the skills to be social or are too fearful to relate to others. It is important to ascertain the difference, and to get the child whatever help he needs to make the choice. No one ever outgrows the need to relate to others in meaningful, caring ways.

"He that raises a large family does, indeed, stand a broader mark for sorrow; but then he stands a broader mark for pleasure too."

Benjamin Franklin

"There is never jealousy where there is not strong regard."

Washington Irving

"Every individual has a place to fill in the world and is important in some respect whether he chooses to be so or not."

Nathaniel Hawthorne

"Treat people as if they were what they ought to be and you help them to become what they are capable of being."

Johann W. von Goethe

"Family life is too intimate to be preserved by the spirit of justice. It can be sustained by a spirit of love which goes beyond justice."

Reinhold Niebuhr

CHAPTER IX

SIBLING RELATIONSHIPS

With each addition of a member, the relationships in a family change. Dependencies, responsibilities, authority, "pecking order" and other expectations — some trivial, some central — are altered for each member.

In families with gifted children some parents report that relationships among siblings can be particularly difficult and frustrating, while others have noted that an astute, mentally quick child can make sibling relationships especially enjoyable. What makes the difference? What are some things that might be helpful to know in dealing with gifted siblings? Although we don't claim to be the *Parents' Complete Guide* in this complex area, we hope the following information will be helpful.

Birth Order

Several studies have found that first-born children usually receive the most attention for the longest time, are high achievers, and are thus more easily identified as gifted (Boroson, 1973; Sutton-Smith & Rosenberg, 1970). The eldest child is likely to be serious, sensitive, conscientious and eager for adult approval. Parents have a special relationship with the first-born, usually expecting more from him, spending more time with him, hoping that this child will model after them (Sutton-Smith & Rosenberg, 1970). For a time this child identified only with adults, while the parents had only this child to represent them in the world.

The second-born child is less adult-oriented, more likely to be peer-oriented. He may value achievement less, show himself less anxious to please his parents, and may reach out to the world more, seeming friendlier and more open. Parents are generally more relaxed in their handling of later-born children, spending less time with them and investing less of their own ego in them (Sutton-Smith & Rosenberg, 1970).

Where there is a middle child, he may feel that his place in the family is uncertain. The youngest child has a unique place because he is the "baby," the first-born has his advantages, but the middle child may feel neglected, discouraged and "squeezed out." (Stoltz, 1975).

Special Roles

Children seek out significant roles within the family. As each child strives for her own place of importance, she watches the others to detect where they succeed or fail. In light of these observations, she evaluates herself and looks for a unique position. If one child adopts a role such as "the outdoorsman," or "the mechanic," "the clown," or "the helpful one," another sibling is unlikely to lay claim to that role, even if the role is one she is capable of playing. Competition can be keen. Often, if one sibling succeeds, the other gives up. If one falters and shows a weakness, another frequently jumps in to demonstrate her own comparative strength. Natural differences between siblings in interests, abilities, personality or temperament may be exaggerated by this competition for roles.

I'm Better Than You Are!

When children compare themselves to their siblings, they may feel less valued, less completely accepted. This is the basis for the familiar sibling rivalry. In some cases the rivalry can be intense and can show itself in really obnoxious behaviors! If such a situation develops in your family, it helps to remember that children are rivals for something they value or prize. You need to discover what it is that is sought so intensely. Some children compete to assure themselves of their personal power, but the rewards siblings more often compete for are praise, attention and special recognition, especially from their parents.

Gifted children are adept at calling attention to themselves, whether consciously or unconsciously. They may be subtle in their demands, they may act more "adult" in style and values, they may be more creative, or just generally more active. In addition, they are usually highly verbal and may engage your attention to the extent that you have less time for other siblings. If your gifted child is also the oldest, it may be a double blow to younger brothers and sisters, as they seldom, if ever have had your undivided attention for long periods of time. If you have an *exceptionally* gifted child, a great deal of attention may be needed to deal with the problem of providing a suitable education, while the others may see that you consider "plain school" good enough for them. Siblings are quick to recognize the unequal attention accorded the gifted child.

Particularly as he gets older, the gifted child may become the organizing force in a family, the virtual head of the household. Because he appears so competent and knowledgeable, parents may relinquish control of the family decision-making process, allowing that child to choose where the family takes vacations, how much money is spent in certain areas, etc. Even when this takeover is not allowed overtly, the diversity and intensity of the gifted child's interests require so much attention and energy that there may be little left over to support the interests of the other family members. Subtly, even subconsciously, parents tend to over-invest in their gifted child, prizing his achievements so highly that their own egos become attached to the child's accomplishments. They may see the child as satisfying their own hopes and dreams.

I'm Not As Good As You Are!

Both the parents and the gifted child himself may regard other siblings as less capable or responsible. This view carries over to the siblings, who doubt their worth and their value to the family. Seeing themselves as "nongifted," they are likely to express resentment toward other family members, either directly or indirectly.

Please be aware that though the younger siblings may not have been identified as gifted, they may have genuine gifts that have not been recognized. They may not have had an opportunity to show their gifts or talents, they may be "late-bloomers," they may be gifted in nonverbal ways that are not so easily measurable, or they may feel that the role of "gifted child" is already taken in the family and so refuse to compete for it. Do not be too quick to conclude that younger siblings are not gifted, or even that they are less gifted. You might wish to consider individual psychological testing. Usually less is expected of younger children, so they may have no chance to show their capabilities. When the gifted high achiever is the first-born, as is often the case, parents may expect the later-born children to exhibit the same traits and characteristics. If these children do not measure up in some areas of achievement, it is easy for parents to overlook their actual strengths and abilities.

For example, math/science achievers may be more readily identifiable than young humanists, so even siblings with specifically intellectual gifts may go unrecognized. If the first-born is a whiz in math, a second-born poet may be thought to be less bright. When siblings do *not* show intellectual gifts, it is important to remember that there are many valuable strengths. A child may have the gift of extraordinary empathy and gentleness with people or animals, or may be a born diplomat, able to defuse strong emotions and ease confrontations. Every child has some special abilities that can be identified and openly valued!

Negative Comparisons

It is important, then, to avoid comparing achievements. Comparisons have negative effects — sometimes on the siblings, sometimes on the gifted child. Questions like "Why aren't you invited to birthday parties and sleep-overs as often as your brother?" or "Why can't you get out there and play soccer with the other kids the way your sister does?" are as damaging as "Why don't you work hard enough to get grades as good as Jane's?" or "How come we can't depend on you the way we do on Bill?" Children are aware of their differences, so parents need to help them see that those differences are natural and to be expected, always supporting strengths rather than emphasizing weaknesses.

While you may be able to avoid comparisons yourself, you will not be able to keep others from making them. Often grandparents, aunts, uncles and family friends make careless comments that hurt the children and fuel sibling rivalry. Wherever possible, since these are people you can presumably talk to, enlist their assistance in stressing the positive and avoiding negative comparisons. This can be a challenge, but it is reasonable to insist that in your family *you* set the house rules and you will not tolerate actions or comments that are harmful to your children. Others — teachers, coaches, your children's peers and acquaintances — will be entirely out of your control. You can compensate for their criticisms and negative comparisons by liberally using praise and encouragement for each child's strengths. This constant and public acknowledgement of *valuable individuality* reassures each child of her own worth and lessens the need to compete destructively with siblings.

Sibling Anger and Depression

Parents become aware of sibling rivalry because it is usually acted out in overt ways, with selfish or spiteful behavior, tattling, bossing others, getting into each other's possessions, embarrassing, criticizing, blaming and engaging in outright physical conflict. Despite the difficulty of doing so, it is important to look behind these behaviors to the underlying purposes. Acting out may be an attempt to get attention, whether negative or positive. Or behavior that appears to be motivated by anger may be a "depressive-equivalent." The anger may cover underlying depression based on the child's sense that he is uncared for, left out or lonely. Sensing the feelings beneath the behavior allows you to respond to the behavior more appropriately, dealing not only with the current fight, but with the child's need for a valued place in the family.

A less obvious expression or rivalry may be modeling behavior. A child may model on the sibling she believes to be most blessed by parental esteem and attention. Or the child may model her behavior after a parent in an attempt to gain value in the parent's eyes. Usually, this modeling is desirable, as it represents one way for the child to learn new ways of being. It may be a normal and appropriate phase of growing up. However, when such modeling is extreme, it may indicate that the child finds nothing of value in her own identity. She may feel that to exist within a family where she is not accepted or appreciated, she dare not be herself.

How Were You As a Sibling?

When trying to analyze the reasons for intense sibling rivalry, parents may need to examine the roles they played in their own families as they were growing up. Gifted children often have gifted parents and unfavorable family patterns may be repeated. As a child, were you "the good one," or "the clown," "the helpful one" or "the smart one?" How did your role help or hinder you and your siblings? Do you expect these family roles and sibling relations to continue into your present family with your children? Are you reacting to the roles of your children as you reacted to roles your brothers and sisters chose? By increasing your self-awareness, you may be able to understand and accept your own reactions and peculiarities and then better understand the attempts of your children to relate to each other.

Other Role Models

Outside influences and role models may also contribute to sibling rivalry and provide children with negative coping behaviors. Parents, TV, teachers and movies offer the primary role models, showing children how family members relate to each other. Unfortunately, too many of these adult role models demonstrate examples of selfishness, insults, sarcasm, revenge and insensitivity instead of showing how to handle relationships in caring ways. It takes positive action by parents to overcome the destructiveness of these models. Unsavory television shows or movies can be replaced as much as possible with other activities. Parents need to express their displeasure at examples of harmful interactions, and should discuss with their children the effects of those interactions.

Handling Squabbles

What can you do in the face of squabbling, picking, fighting or other negative sibling behaviors, whatever their cause? One general rule is to refuse as far as possible to become part of the competition. Whenever you become involved in your children's fights, you reinforce the behavior that caught your attention, and encourage its repetition. Unless the situation is physically harmful, you can stay out of it. Your withdrawal conveys your belief that the children are capable of handling the situation themselves.

This does not mean you should ignore such behaviors entirely, particularly if they are continuous and develop a pattern that may be especially harmful to one or more of the children. There is a difference between allowing yourself to be pulled into specific confrontations and setting overall standards of conduct. We would encourage you to be openly caring and active. Let your children know that you expect them to behave reasonably to each other and that you do not tolerate cruelty. Remind them of the ways they are dependent on each other and encourage sensitivity. One approach could be, "I feel sad when you make fun of your sister, because I know you also depend on her to help you learn new cheers."

When taking a strong stand against unacceptable behavior, beware of being over-critical and punitive. Parental harshness generally leads to even greater rivalry among siblings because the children are less confident of their acceptance. When children are made to feel insecure and guilty, they may desperately compete to reassure themselves that they are equal to their siblings. As always, try to recognize and accept the feelings that underly the behavior even though you must criticize the behavior.

Broaden the Roles

It may also help to overtly label whatever positive roles a child has assumed. It is important to find several different roles to label, to show the child that he is capable of making many different contributions to the family. Today he may be "the finder," next week "the rescuer," or "the handyman." Remember to provide labels for alternative roles for the gifted child to assure him that he has non-intellectual traits that are also important and necessary. In this way the children can broaden their concepts of themselves and perhaps come to realize that some roles can be shared with siblings without harm to any of them.

Some roles carry less prestige than others. A child may feel that being "the handyman" just cannot compete with being "the organizer," or "the planner." In such a case, it may be helpful to point out the component parts of a role. Just as "housewife" may take on greater prestige when the role is shown to include accountant, personnel manager, chauffeur, chef, maintenance person, etc., "handyman" may be more acceptable if you label traits that are necessary to it. Organization, perserverance, creativity and dexterity may confer more value on the role.

Sibling Synergy

As each child learns to have confidence in her own identity, she can begin to encourage the others to develop theirs. The result can be what we refer to as "sibling synergy," a positive force. "Synergy" allows the whole to be greater than the sum of its parts because of the interaction of the parts. What neither sibling could achieve alone may be achieved by their working together. Whenever possible, encourage your children to be synergetic rather than competitive. The influence of siblings can be very powerful and synergy can affect the family as a whole. The key is to find ways to harness that power for positive goals.

Please note that sibling companionship goes hand-in-hand with sibling rivalry. Children do not compete twenty-four hours a day. Much of the time they may be friends and companions, and some children with strong egos may actually thrive on competition, in spite of being basically compatible. The goal, as we see it, is to promote cooperation and companionship as much as possible and to reduce whatever competition seems to threaten a child's sense of well-being and personal importance.

Family Equilibrium

Family patterns, where characteristic roles are available to each child, are reassuring. Everyone has his own "turf," and each member of the family can count on the others to play their traditional roles. Predictability is part of what makes family life comfortable. Particularly when each member feels valued and accepted, the family unit functions smoothly. It is as if each family member is a planet following a separate orbit, independent of the others but influencing their orbits to keep the whole system in order. A stable equilibrium is reached within the family.

Events do occur, however, that disrupt the equilibrium. Illness, a new job, a move, a change in schools, divorce, remarriage, etc. can each create disequilibrium that may last three to nine months. During this period of readjustment, when old ways are threatened, new ways are being tried. Sibling rivalry may become particularly intense as brothers and sisters test each other, sometimes trying to find new roles, sometimes trying to cling to the familiar ones. Though a new equilibrium will be established and a new pattern created, the family's patience may be sorely tried in the process. The new pattern may be very similar to the old or very different; it may be healthier and more satisfying or less healthy. The quality of the new equilibrium depends on how matters are handled during the disruptive crisis.

Such an upsetting period can be, therefore, a time of opportunity. It allows family members to try new roles and new behaviors that under the old conditions were unthinkable. They can come to find new value in themselves, discovering new ways of being appreciated by others. One colleague compared the period of disequilibrium to a man standing on one foot. If you push him gently in one direction, he will fall; if you push him gently in the other direction, he plants both feet firmly on the ground. Perhaps you can be that gentle push in your family, using the troubled period as an opportunity to broaden the range of roles and activities your children allow themselves to try. Assure them that their basic security is still there, that the family is still a unit, however different it may seem, while encouraging them to consider new possibilities. Meanwhile, let them see that they do not have to waste their energies competing intensely for your affection. That should be always a given!

During the periods of family stress or periods of calm, the principle to keep in mind is that each child needs to feel loved and accepted, valued and needed. Stressing strengths, avoiding negative comparisons, refusing to tolerate insensitivity, giving special attention to each child (use "special time" as discussed in Chapter VII), and trying to provide positive role models in your own relationships can all help to minimize the negative impact of sibling rivalry, and promote sibling synergy.

172

References

Boroson, W. First-Born-Fortune's Favorite? *Annual Editions: Readings in Human Development, '73–'74.* Guilford, Ct.: The Dushkin Publishing Group, 1973, 193-196.

Soltz, V. *Articles of Supplementary Reading for Parents.* Chicago: Alfred Adler Institute, 1975.

Sutton-Smith, B. and Rosenberg, B.G. *The Sibling.* N.Y.: Holt, Rinehart and Winston, Inc., 1970.

Some Frequent Questions About Sibling Relationships

How can I help my nongifted children feel proud of their lower school grades?

You can start by increasing your own sensitivity so that you avoid the "either-or" trap — a child is either gifted or not. Like most things in life, it is more a matter of how much giftedness a child has and in what areas. There is no such thing as a "nongifted" child. It will be up to you to help each child identify at least one, and we hope several, areas in his life where he is special or talented. Each child should be expected to work at a level reasonably close to his potential in school and in other areas. Children of average intelligence have the ability to do at least passing level work in most schools until they reach high school or perhaps college — provided they are motivated and willing to spend a reasonable amount of time at their work. Thus, they, too, can obtain good grades, although they will have

to work harder to do so than someone who is intellectually gifted. In a similar fashion, a less gifted child may have a particular
talent for singing, for mechanics, or for dealing with animals
or with people, whereas the intellectually gifted person may
have to work harder in these areas to achieve at the same level.
You should make your children aware that many kinds of highly
valued behavior exist other than just intellectual abilities measured by grades.

**One of my children was very outgoing and the other was
quite reserved. All of a sudden they have reversed roles.
Is this normal?**

Yes, this happens, particularly with twins. Often there is
some clear event that stimulates the reversal, such as an illness
in one of the children. It is as though one child laid claim to a
particular role in the family and the other child was unwilling
to challenge that role until a particular opportunity arose or
until the other child gave up the role by moving into a new
developmental stage. With gifted children you seem to find more
role reversals since they try so many different kinds of behaviors.

**My kids seem to pick at each other all the time! Where do
I start to help them change this?**

Listen and watch carefully to see what they are being rivals
for. Often it is for their parents' attention or for power. Look at
the kinds of situations where you give them attention. Most
parents discover that their attention is given to the children most
often when they are misbehaving — and only rarely when they
are quiet and cooperating. Change your pattern so that they
receive more attention for cooperating and playing nicely.

During those all too rare times when they are quiet and coopera-tive, tell them how much you appreciate it. Or you can say some-thing like "your cooperation has allowed me to get my work done, so how about if we have some ice cream." Some parents have found it helps to keep a few balloons or pieces of sugarless gum in their pocket to shower on the siblings when they are being pleasant with each other.

During the actual squabbling, you might try several things. If nagging seems clearly intended for you to hear, remove yourself. Go to the back yard with a book. If, upon re-entering the house, the nagging starts again, go back outside without comment. Some parents have bought stereo earphones to put on when the squabbling begins. Others have taken a peaceful, solitary drive in the car. The point is, try to avoid getting involved unneces-sarily, and remember to give each child frequent, brief special time.

How tolerant should I be in letting my children settle arguments and fights on their own, especially when the older, brighter one usually wins?

As mentioned above, you should probably be pretty tolerant. However, it would be helpful to help the children involved develop appreciation for how the older one feels. This can be done through role-playing, and role-reversal, along with ex-perimentally playing out some non-argumentative ways of solv-ing problems. This will not likely be effective in the heat of the moment, however, and you may have to intervene to send all children to their rooms or neutral corners for a cooling off period. Over time you probably can shape their behavior so that they become more diplomatic and empathetic with each other's position. And, of course, the parents must be quite aware of how they settle their own disagreements in front of the children — what role models they are providing — for it is in this way that children learn a great deal about resolving tensions with persons close to them.

Is it possible that an 18 month old child we believe to be gifted could feel sibling rivalry?

It is not only possible; it is probable. Gifted children tend to hit developmental stages earlier than most children. This heightened awareness of what they want and of the behaviors of others makes them more likely to compete intensely.

Is there really anything to "middle child" problems?

Yes, there is. The oldest child often receives more pressures to achieve, and is more oriented toward adult activities. Perhaps this is why so many identified gifted children are first-born. The youngest child often has the role of the "baby of the family." The middle child may get lost, without a special role in the family. Gifted middle children may be difficult to identify and have some particular problems in finding an identity and a sense of self-worth.

"Tradition is an important help to history, but its statements should be carefully scrutinized before we rely on them."

Joseph Addison

"An old error is always more popular than a new truth."

German Proverb

"The custom and fashion of today will be the awkwardness and outrage of tomorrow — so arbitrary are these transient laws."

Alexandre Dumas

"The important thing is not to stop questioning."

Albert Einstein

"Since when was genius found respectable?"

Elizabeth Barrett Browning

"There are only two lasting bequests we could hope to give our children. One of these is roots; the other is wings."

Hodding Carter

CHAPTER X

TRADITION BREAKING

We live in a world governed by tradition, from the smallest matter of proper dress or table manners to the largest issue of moral principle. Some traditions affect entire cultures or large portions of society, providing cohesion, integration, and a predictable basis for a whole social system. Laws, codes of ethics, religious rituals, moral codes and formal ceremonies solidify and maintain these traditions. Other traditions affect smaller groups within a society — ethnic minorities, geographical groups, the sexes, members of particular age groups, families, clubs, etc. These, too, may be expressed in customs, manners, written and unwritten rules, and rituals. When we carry on traditions, we pass values, goals, history and feelings from person to person, group to group, or generation to generation. By doing so, we reaffirm our commitment to the others who share that tradition. Traditions help to provide structure for our lives, to define our values, even to form our dreams, as they help us to know what others may expect of us.

A Foundation of Shared Experiences

In order to feel part of the world around us, we need a basic tap root — a root that goes deep into the shared experiences of our culture. This root gives us a sense of security and belonging as we undertake risky ventures into the outside world. For children, this tap root is usually set firmly in family traditions, in the intense history of shared experiences with family members. As the child grows, he also sends out lateral roots by interacting with others from different backgrounds. These, too, provide security and a sense of belonging to a broader group, of becoming integrated into the world.

Rites of Passage

Many traditions, rituals and customs are related to specific stages of development, changing or being discarded as the child grows. When a child begins school, for instance, a completely new set of rituals must be learned and dealt with, while others — the afternoon nap, perhaps — are left behind. There are many "rites of passage" designed to mark new stages of development, some of them cultural, others recognized within the family or other small group. Certain birthdays (13, 16, 18, 21) may be marked as special occasions, or moving from elementary to middle school or junior high school to high school. Reaching these stages means reorganizing life to a greater or lesser extent, adjusting to new expectations, to new friends, to the loss of old comforts (or pains) and the gaining of new ones. Sometimes new expectations are clearly marked — the sixteen year old learns to drive — but others must be figured out by watching carefully what others are doing — the junior high crowd may wear only one brand of shoe!

Sometimes Traditions Do Not Fit

Gifted children may have problems with traditions in several ways. Because they typically go through stages of mental and physical development faster, they may be out of phase with the rituals and traditions that fit their age. The expectations of society do not fit the child as an individual. They seem to reach the "terrible twos" and the "incredible Oedipal" stages earlier than normal, for instance, and may already be involved in a variety of social activities by the age of six or eight. Rituals designed for kindergarten and first grade children to help provide a transition from the small world of family to the larger world of other children and new adults, may seem babyish, trivial and totally unnecessary to the gifted child. Throughout their childhoods, they must handle a number of rituals earlier than other children.

In addition, gifted children move more rapidly through what have been called the "Stages of Moral Development" (Kohlberg, 1964), summarized in Table 10. This rapid movement means that the gifted child is likely to be out of step with many of the needs, preferences, even personality traits of his age peers. He is, therefore, likely to question, challenge or defy traditions that his peers take for granted.

Only about 10% of all people reach the last two stages of moral development. In our experience, though, most gifted children do achieve these upper levels unless their environment has prevented such growth. People in these upper levels are the leaders, creators and inventors who make major contributions to society and who help reformulate knowledge and philosophy, often changing major traditions in the process. While traditions form a continuum from the most insignificant matter of social custom to the principles formed into law, they may also go beyond law, to sweeping principles of universal order. Those who have reached the highest levels of moral development may go beyond the law as well, sometimes sacrificing themselves and often changing the world's perception of the law, and finally the law itself. Gifted children may set themselves on such a course early in life.

180

Table 10

Stages of Moral Development
(Adapted from Kohlberg, 1964)

Stage	Issue of Moral Concern
Selfish Obedience	
I	Rules followed to avoid punishment; obedience and concern for physical consequences.
II	Doing things for others because it will result in others doing things in return; concern for reward, equal sharing and benefit to self.
Conforming to Traditions	
III	Whatever pleases the majority is considered morally right; other viewpoints can be seen, conformity is prized, desire to do things for others.
IV	Group authority, law, duty and rules of society prized; concern for maintaining social order for its own sake; social disapproval avoided; emphasis on the inherent "rightness" of rules and duties.
Moral Principles Beyond Conformity	
V	Internal commitment to principles of personal conscience; concern with individual rights within standards set by consensus; emphasis on fair procedures for reaching consensus and for evaluating principles and rules.
VI	Concern with universal ethical principles and abstract morality affecting all beings regardless of conventional views; emphasis on universality, consistency and logical comprehensiveness.

Asking "Why?"

Blind belief, unquestioning obedience or passive acceptance of traditions conflicts with the nature of the gifted child, who continually asks, "Why?" No custom or ritual seems exempt from the gifted child's critical evaluation. "Why do I have to stand up when an older person comes into the room, even if I'm working on something important?" "Why does the neatness of my handwriting count, as long as you can read it?" "What difference does it make whether I wear jeans or a skirt, as long as I'm covering my body?" "Why can't girls be generals and boys sell lipstick?" "Why do politicians make promises they won't be able to keep?"

Some of the traditions that help keep society running smoothly and predictably may be little more than habit, retained not for their necessity or value, but simply because they have never been examined and discarded. Worse, some of them actually stifle the individual, cutting off avenues of development that should be open to all, simply because an earlier, less enlightened era decreed it so. The child with exceptional analytical ability can and probably should question and reject many of these useless, empty, sometimes harmful customs.

Breaking Established Patterns

As bright children grow, they become aware of alternatives and begin to realize that they need not be bound by traditions. We believe that this personal freedom should be encouraged for the child's sake, even though it may cause some discomfort for the parents. Gifted children need to know that each person may change his choices when the old ones are no longer fulfilling, that expanding his world is a reasonable goal. We suggest that you help your child optimistically assess new possibilities. As he learns of traditions other than his own, he also becomes aware of alternative life styles that may be more fulfilling. The more experiences he has, the more skills he will acquire and the more options he will find open to him. This allows him greater control over his life.

Of course, you will not want to encourage your children to break traditions just for the sake of breaking them, though many children do this as a way to establish an identity separate from their family. Remind them that many, if not all, traditions serve a definite purpose. Try to help them discover that purpose and examine it carefully, weighing it against the gains they expect to get from rejecting the old ways. There is always a trade-off, and a child should understand that trade-off before acting. He may discard all table manners, for instance, but may discover that no one wants to eat with him any more. He may go to a job interview in cut-offs and a dirty tee shirt, but he is likely to come away jobless. Help him see traditions not only from his own viewpoint, but from the viewpoint of others who may consider them important.

How Much Does It Cost?

Breaking tradition is a two-edged sword. On one side it promotes independence and creative thinking. On the other side, it may so irritate or alienate those for whom traditions are helpful, that the child may find himself isolated and alone, having severed his connection with his group.

Many people think in absolute terms, considering everything "good" or "evil," "proper" or "improper," with no middle ground and no room for question. Gifted children go beyond this exclusive thinking unless they have been forcibly convinced that questioning authority is not allowed. Their divergent thinking allows them to integrate ideas and information instead of compartmentalizing, to make new connections and devise new principles. They may wish to substitute these principles immediately for older traditions. But social and cultural changes are occurring so rapidly today that many people have been driven to cling ever more steadfastly to their familiar customs and rules, in an effort to alleviate their discomfort. They are likely to be particularly hostile to those who seem to threaten their security. Most authorities, when directly challenged, harden their positions and become even less tolerant. Gifted children should be taught that it may be self-defeating to push so hard or confront so directly that authorities take a stand prematurely to merely assert their control.

The costs of tradition breaking are not exclusively a matter of the reactions of others. Breaking a tradition the child has previously upheld, believed in or even passively accepted, puts her in a state of crisis. She is likely to feel awkward, unsure and vulnerable. She may realize that by publicly breaking the tradition, she is permanently affecting her relationship with others. Whether their reactions are positive or negative, her place with them will never be the same. There is also the conflict between the safety of the known and the adventure of the unknown. It is easy to stick with what you know, however unsatisfying; it takes courage and self-confidence to attempt something new.

Extra Understanding and Patience

Gifted children need extra understanding because they are likely to be caught in this conflict over how far they may go in questioning or discarding customs without threatening their own security or sense of belonging. Attempting to provide that understanding and support their need to evaluate their world for themselves can be difficult for parents. It is said that young Albert Schweitzer, seeing that other boys could not afford warm clothes, refused to wear the clothes his parents managed to provide on the limited income of a country pastor. He insisted on dressing as poorly as the others, much to his parents' chagrin and embarrassment. For him, the principle of equality was more important than his parents' determination that he observe the social proprieties. It was a conflict they never, apparently, resolved (Manton, 1955).

Perhaps the hardest part of parenting a gifted child is that you cannot hide. He will confront you with your hypocrisies, find fallacies, locate loopholes. One seven year old asked his mother, "Is that a *real* law or one like the 55 mph speed limit?" You cannot pretend that inconsistencies do not exist either within the family or within society. Often, you will be unable to defend some irrational customs. You may discover that many of your own traditions have been maintained unthinkingly, once your child confronts you with them. Is it really necessary to make the bed each morning, or wear a tie, or run the vacuum cleaner every day, or invite someone to dinner whose company you do not enjoy? Your child may be developing different values, but are those values necessarily worse than yours? As a result of your child's questions, you may suddenly realize that your own life has been scheduled by rituals and that your "life plan" is going nowhere; it may be difficult, though healthy, to share portions of your discovery with your child.

What Are the Family's Traditions?

It may be helpful for you to *examine your family's cultural beliefs, customs, traditions, values, preconceptions and prejudices.* Doing this as a family shows the children that you allow the questioning of traditions and lets you model socially acceptable means of doing it. Then, together, you can define your priorities. Using the values clarification exercises mentioned in Chapter IV, decide which customs are essential for your well-being and the well-being of the family as a whole. What traditions are sacred and cannot be broken or violated without causing major

disruption in the family? When you make these choices, you
give the children fair warning and provide them a chance (if
they insist on challenging even the sacred traditions) to present
their views as gently, as diplomatically as possible.

In this process you *provide them an example,* encouraging them
to go through the same process for themselves, to set their own
value priorities, to make choices. You may find yourself helping
them when a situation arises simply by prompting them to see
their choices clearly. For example, a nine year old saw it was
raining one morning. "I'll get soaked!" she complained. "Nobody — *but nobody* — wears raincoats this year!"

"Do you like getting wet?" her mother asked.

"No. You have to sit all day feeling damp and cold and —
muggy. Yuck!"

"But the other kids would tease you if you wore your raincoat?"

"Sure. I told you, *nobody* wears them!" The girl stood looking
at the rain while her mother said nothing. "Aw, the heck with it.
I don't care what they say, it's just stupid to get wet!" She put on
her raincoat and set off for school.

Open discussions can help a gifted child develop a greater
understanding of peer relations, sibling relations, the need for
discipline, etc. At the same time, you may learn much about the
functioning of your family. You might consider some of the
following questions: How does your family reward creative,
analytical thinking? Does your family prefer conformity instead?
How do you assure your children that they are able to decide
whether an idea is true or reasonable? How do you assure them
they can act on those decisions? How much of the family's time
is spent in meaningless rituals and habits? How do you react
when traditions are questioned by a family member or when
you encounter others with different traditions? How do you
help your children to appreciate the value of their traditions

while encouraging them to avoid being imprisoned by them? The answers to these questions may surprise you and may encourage you to make some changes. Finally, there is the most difficult of the questions. What do you do, or will you do, when tradition breaking gets serious, when a child wants to try something harmful or illegal or with long-term consequences? It is then that a clear set of priorities is indispensable!

Help your child be aware that tradition breaking causes discomfort in others, but that they may not understand why they are uncomfortable or angry. The gifted child's empathy will help him appreciate that when he confronts the traditions of others, this should be done as gently, sensitively and politely as possible.

We hope that you will remember that patience, tolerance and resiliency will be your greatest allies in your attempt to maintain both the security of the old ways and the freedom to look for better ways. Recognize that you have the power to establish traditions because they are important to you.

References

Kohlberg, L. Development of moral character and moral ideology. In M.L. Hoffman and L.W. Hoffman (Eds.), *Review of Child Development Research, Vol. I.* N.Y.: Russell Sage, 1964.

Manton, J. *The Story of Albert Schweitzer.* N.Y.: Abelard Schuman, 1955.

Some Frequent Questions
About Traditions

My child always seems to challenge authority and wants to be different. I'm afraid he's going to be very unpopular, that he might drop out or get into serious trouble. What can I do?

Challenging authority is usual for gifted children, particularly as they approach teenage years. However, whenever we hear "always," we feel compelled to question it. Are there not *some* authorities he seems willing to accept? Perhaps these provide something to build on. In those situations where he does question authority, you may, to a large degree, have to allow "natural consequences" to occur. You can help him see how his behavior may eventually harm him, discussing it with him in non-threatening ways and accepting his feelings. You may be able to help him appreciate the value of traditions even while giving him the freedom to question them. For example, if he decides that being polite is unnecessary, you may have to recognize the fact that you cannot force him to be polite. You may, however, allow (or arrange for) consequences which might lead to a discussion of the reasons for courtesy. If you were to abolish all courtesy in the family for a period of time — perhaps exaggerating the opposite — everyone might come to an appreciation of the effect of manners on human interaction.

Obviously, there are some traditions, such as laws, where you cannot allow natural consequences to occur. You cannot allow your child to endanger himself or others. In these cases you might be able to help the child explore the origins and current purposes of the tradition in his own mind, and anticipate the consequences mentally rather than facing those consequences in reality after acting in a way he cannot take back.

My child has rejected all of our family's and society's traditions. Won't this make her feel more alienated from society?

Has she really rejected them *all?* Is so, it would be most unusual, and professional help would seem to be indicated. Whether she has rejected all, or just most, it sounds as if communications have seriously broken down within the family, and that anger, depression and alienation are present. Unless she can accommodate herself to some traditions and accept their value, she will indeed feel increasingly alienated. You can help by examining whether you or other family members are putting too much emphasis on trivial rituals rather than those traditions that contribute importantly to meaningful human relations. Try going back to communicating feelings (see Chapter VII) since communication, sharing of feelings and trust are the basic underpinnings of meaningful traditions.

How can I encourage tradition-breaking? My gifted children seem very conformist and overly concerned with doing things the "right" way.

There is a feeling of safety in staying with familiar behaviors and traditions. Since traditional matters are so predictable, there is a sense of being in control of your destiny — though that may be a false sense. Children who are overly conforming often fear that dire consequences might occur if they were non-conformist. In addition to reassuring and encouraging your children, it may help if *you* occasionally act in unexpected, non-traditional ways. You might, yourself, openly raise questions about the purposes of specific traditions, along with asking aloud what would be the worst thing that might happen if it were broken. Do not forget to reward your children for their expressions of novelty and creativity, and accept their beginning attempts at independence even if they are faltering steps.

"The pain of the mind is worse than the pain of the body."

P. Syrus

"The whole conviction of my life now rests upon the belief that loneliness, far from being a rare and curious phenomenon, peculiar to myself and to a few other solitary men, is the central and inevitable fact of human existence."

Thomas Wolfe

"It is foolish to tear one's hair in grief, as if grief could be lessened by baldness."

Cicero

"People are lonely because they build walls instead of bridges."

Joseph F. Newton

"The most immutable barrier in nature is between one man's thoughts and another's."

William James

"A problem well-stated is a problem half-solved."

Charles Kettering

"The world is so full of care and sorrow that it is a gracious debt we owe to one another to discover the bright crystals of delight hidden in somber circumstances and irksome tasks."

Helen Keller

"Who will tell whether one happy moment of love, or the joy of breathing or walking on a bright morning and smelling the fresh air, is not worth all the suffering and effort which life implies?"

Erich Fromm

CHAPTER XI

DEPRESSION

Are gifted children more likely than other children to get depressed? Are they more likely to attempt suicide? We think the answer to the first question is "yes" and to the second, "perhaps." We also believe that it does not have to be that way — you can take definite steps to reduce the likelihood of depression, or at least to lessen its intensity.

How Serious a Problem Is It?

The seriousness of depression in gifted children must not be overlooked. In the past two decades suicides among young persons have increased 250%, and suicide is cited as the third leading cause of death in the United States for persons between the ages of 15 and 24 (Lajole & Shore, 1981). Suicide attempts may occur more frequently among youths who are unusually creative (Bowers, 1978), have better than average grades (Fox, 1971; Lester & Lester, 1971), attend highly competitive and selective schools (Lester & Lester, 1971; Ross, 1969; Seiden, 1969), and whose college grade point average recently declined (Seiden, 1969).

While it is true that not all depression ends in suicide, these data serve to alert us to the extent of the problem. No matter how unpleasant a subject depression may be, parents must consider it if they wish to provide guidance for their gifted children.

What Is Depression?

As we use it here, the term "depression" is more than mild sadness. Depression refers to intense feelings of despair, guilt, hopelessness, and a sense of worthlessness. A depressed person recognizes that things are not as they should be, but feels helpless to correct the situation.

It is the sense of hopelessness, the feeling that "all is lost," that makes depression particularly difficult to overcome. There is neither the energy nor the desire to take action and make changes. The feelings involved in depression are vague and diffuse, seemingly timeless. A depressed person feels as if he has always felt depressed and always will.

It often surprises parents to learn that children can be depressed as well as adults. Even infants and toddlers can be depressed, a disorder that can cause physical problems in growth and development if the child does not receive affection and care. Both in children and adults, depression is usually accompanied by withdrawal, lowered energy, narrowing of interests, and perhaps by sleep disturbances, over-eating, or a loss of appetite.

Three Kinds of Depression

There are three different kinds of depression that gifted children are likely to experience. One comes from their desire to live up to standards of morality, responsibility and achievement that they may have set impossibly high (see Chapter VI). As one gifted teenager said "I become sad . . . I doze and hope to dream of fulfilling my ideal. Ideal what? Ideal anything! I have so many unattainable ideals I could turn into reality" (American Association for Gifted Children, 1978).

Another type of depression may come from feeling alienated, cut off from other people. They may feel that others accept them not as persons, but only as brains, computers or achievers. These children may begin to relate to people only in superficial ways, revealing only what they think others expect from them, only what others are likely to accept, sensing all along their own hypocrisy (Miller, 1981).

A third type, "existential depression," stems from their intense concerns about the basic problems of human existence. They are likely to worry about whether human values are no more than situational, whether they are arbitrary and unreal (May, 1953). Underneath such abstract concerns as whether life has any absolute meaning there is usually the personal worry about the meaning of the child's own life.

These three types of depression are similar — all have underlying feelings of anger. A basic principle for understanding depression — your own or someone else's — is to become aware of the anger involved. Anger is a feeling most of us can understand; it leads to action. When we deny our anger, pretend it does not exist, we are likely to become depressed. Depression can be thought of as anger with "no place to go."

Sometimes children feel frustrated and helpless in their anger because they are allowed neither an outlet for expressing their feelings nor a say in changing the situation that is making them angry. Sometimes the anger underlying depression is directed at the self. Children may blame or even punish themselves for their misdeeds or shortcomings. Sometimes they feel furious with what seems the "unfairness of life," or caught up in a sense of frustration so sweeping and vague that they feel utterly powerless. One parent harshly labeled a variation of this anger a "pity party" — when children are upset at the mistreatment they have received but, rather than seeking a remedy, give themselves large does of pity, continuously mulling over their anger and pouting.

What is seen on the surface is depression; what is underneath is anger. Until a person realizes his anger, dealing with depression is like trying to put smoke in an evelope. Every time he tries to take a handful, it swirls away. Once he re-labels his feelings as anger, he usually experiences a release of energy that enables him to take some action, even if that action is merely to stop blaming or punishing himself.

Wearing a Hair Shirt

Because it is so basic to depression, self-punishment may require elaboration. In the Middle Ages, monks who felt sinful or unworthy sewed themselves into hair shirts, wearing them — hair side inward — for day after day through the hot, dusty countryside. The discomfort, itching and sores that resulted were atonements for the monks' shortcomings. When they felt they had atoned sufficiently, they cut away their hair shirts.

It is easy to say that wearing a hair shirt would not make one a better person. It would neither "undo" an act nor rectify a situation. Yet few of us realize that the self-blame of depression *is* the mental equivalent of wearing a hair shirt. Most of our hair shirts seem to come from setting inappropriate standards for ourselves.

Existential Depression

Most teenagers go through periods of questioning their personal values, examining their relationships with others and searching for "meaning." They may doubt or dispute religious and ethical codes and ask unanswerable question such as, "If

God is all that is good, and if God made everything, where did evil come from and how can God allow it to continue?" This questioning is a normal part of adolescence, but is surprising from an eight or nine year old child. Because it is so unexpected, it may be overlooked, dismissed, and not given the serious consideration it deserves when it comes as early as it may in gifted children. But whenever it comes, existential questioning brings with it a pervasive sense of loneliness, accompanied by depression and anxiety as the child considers the possibilities of life's "nothingness." One six year old had the following conversation:

> Child: "How can I know what it feels like to die?"
>
> Mom: "You can't. Neither can I."
>
> Child: "Only the dead know and they can't talk. (Pause) So I guess I'll have to wait till I die to know what it's like."
>
> Mom: "I guess so. And me too."
>
> Child: "Everyone, even people not in our family — everything has to die."
>
> Mom: "At least everything alive."
>
> Child: "Even things not alive die. Even this table has to die."
>
> Mom: "Maybe, but not quite the same way."
>
> Child: "Yes, even the earth can die. If everything alive died, even things that never lived would die. So there isn't any 'always.' There isn't any always at all!"

Virtually all gifted children have at least one period of existential depression in their lives. To cope with it, they must be able to find meaning in their own lives and in their relations with others. They must develop a sense of belonging in the universe, and that feeling will rely heavily on relationships with family and friends.

Help!

Parents can help their children learn to avoid or cope with these depressions regardless of the type or intensity. The steps outlined below, along with previous advice, should reduce the frequency and intensity of depressions. Ordinarily, they should last no longer than a few hours or days at most. If they continue, *do not hesitate to get professional advice.*

Please do not pass off a child's depression as "a stage," or tell the child to "just snap out of it." Such statements inhibit communication just when she is especially in need of communication. If it were possible to simply "snap out" of a depression, the subject would be of no serious concern, and belittling a child's depression implies lack of respect for her as a person. The depression is both real and painful to the person who experiences it, regardless of age.

Do not try to argue a child out of depression. The more you logically tell him what a deserving child he is, the more he will tell you he is worthless. If he says he is "no good at anything," and you point out that he just won a trophy (or did anything else right), he will almost certainly tell you why that does not count. Even though this approach is ineffective, parents continue to use it because it sometimes *appears* to work. The child stops *talking* about how bad or worthless he is. Unfortunately, in addition to the depression that he continues to feel inside, he now feels that his parents or others do not understand or accept him.

Adopt a posture of "I'm sorry you feel that way," instead of trying to reason the child out of her depression. Help her to re-label her depressed feelings as anger and frustration. You might try a series of statements such as the following: "You sure seem angry at yourself;" "You're really down on yourself — really kicking yourself around the block;" "It looks to me as if you're being judge, jury and prosecutor, with no time off for good behavior." "I really wonder whether punishing yourself this way will change things or make you a better person." Your comments can help the child see that she is punishing herself, and raise questions about how much punishment she really needs. You might even talk about hair shirts and point out that she is the only one who can remove hers, asking her when she thinks she might be ready. It may be that your conversation will end for the time being with "I guess I don't see you as being as bad as you feel you are. I hope you'll feel better about yourself soon."

After such a conversation, give her some time to think; most people cannot give up depression immediately. Note that you are not denying feelings nor that problems exist. You are not announcing that everything always happens for the best and turns out fine. You *are* recognizing her right to her own feelings, enhancing her self-esteem and giving her reassurance about her abilities and worth, while at the same time telling her that you do not support her totally bleak view.

Suicide

The idea that our children might contemplate suicide is monumentally threatening to us as parents. It seems particularly difficult when our children are gifted, when they seem to have everything to live for and seem to have unusual reserves of strength and ability. Why would such a child wish to end his life, the life we have worked so hard to help develop?

Whether a person is gifted or not, suicidal behavior comes primarily from repeated stressful situations with which he feels unable to cope. The anger within the depression grows so great that he finally punishes himself or someone else in the most dramatic way possible. The aspect of anger directed at others should not be overlooked; a suicide may be intended to kill more than one person.

Although gifted children do get depressed and suicide does happen, this does not mean that all gifted children are likely to take their own lives. Though gifted children under age fourteen may talk about suicide, it is, in fact, rare in children of that age. Gestures, suicide attempts or other destructive behavior become more likely between fourteen and nineteen when teenagers face identity crises, trying to find out who they are and where they fit in the world. Drug and alcohol experimentation or abuse increase the likelihood of depression and cloudy thinking (Miller, 1975).

Keys to preventing severe depressions or suicides in gifted children come from earlier chapters on motivation, communication of feelings, discipline, stress management, and peer and sibling relations. We merely extend those chapters when we suggest that you cannot afford to ignore the expression of feelings of loneliness, unhappiness or — particularly — a wish to die. A suicidal gesture is a cry for help; it should not be ignored, minimized or ridiculed. *Professional help is needed.*

. The chances of your child attempting or committing suicide are small. We feel they can be made even smaller by your awareness of the possibility and sensitive handling of depression. Whether within the family or with professional help, sharing of your child's depressed feelings can result in a closer, more supportive emotional relationship.

Grief and Mourning

Reactions of grief and mourning at the loss of a loved one are different from the depressions discussed above, although sometimes persons who are grieving may also be depressed. Grief and mourning are normal, strong feelings of sadness over losing a part of yourself. Depression may accompany grief as anger at "fate," or the "unfairness of life," or perhaps at yourself for something you left unsaid or undone. It is important to allow and encourage the expression of grief. Those who express their grief and openly share it early after a loss usually find an added depth in their relationships with others. Those who suppress it often suffer a delayed reaction that may turn into depression.

Children react to the loss of relatives and friends just as parents do. Even as infants and toddlers, gifted children are keenly aware of their bonding to others, and may intensely react to interruptions of those bonds. The loss need not be caused by death; to these children, separation and divorce can also be interpreted as loss. They *will* respond to such an event, possibly showing their feelings by withdrawal or changes in eating or sleeping patterns.

Parents can see these changes. What they cannot see are the explanations the child may be devising about what is happening in her life. The egocentricity of childhood — and gifted children seem to have particularly large egos — may lead her to center her explanations on herself. She may feel that some misbehavior on *her* part caused the marital separation. It is especially necessary for parents to talk and listen to gifted children in such circumstances. Tell them what is happening and — as far as possible — why. Insert some reality into their fantasies.

Parents Can Get Depressed Too!

The hard work, responsibility and high expectations we have make us, as parents, likely candidates for depression ourselves. We can easily come to feel guilty that we are not doing all we could for our children who have such great potential. We may become frustrated by the indifference or apparent hostility of the rest of the world. We, too, must have an outlet for the angry feelings that support depression.

Make sure that you are meeting your own needs just as conscientiously as you focus on your children's needs. It is easy to let the entire family focus on gifted children, with resulting depression and underlying resentment in you or elsewhere in the family. Virtually all of the points we have raised in this chapter about gifted children apply to you as well, if you take parenting responsibilities seriously. You, too, must beware of setting standards you cannot meet, demanding more of the world than it can give and sewing yourself into a hair shirt. We recognize your needs as we turn to the next chapter on parent relationships.

References

American Association for Gifted Children. *On Being Gifted.* N.Y.: Walker and Co., 1978.

Bowers, P.G. Hypnotizability, creativity and the role of effortless experience. *International Journal of Experimental Hypnosis,* 1978, 26, 184-202.

Fox, R. Today's students: Suicide among students and its prevention. *Royal Society of Health Journal,* 1971, 91, 181-185.

Lajole, S.P. and Shore, B.M. Three myths? The over-representation of the gifted among dropouts, delinquents and suicides. *Gifted Child Quarterly,* 1981, 25, No. 3, 183-243.

Lester, G. and Lester, D. *Suicide: The Gamble with Death.* Englewood, N.J.: Prentice-Hall, 1971.

May, R. *Man's Search for Himself.* N.Y.: Norton, 1953.

Miller, A. *Prisoners of Childhood.* N.Y.: Basic Books, 1981.

Miller, J.P. Suicide and adolescence. *Adolescence,* 1975, 10(37), 11-24.

Seiden, R. Campus tragedy: A study of student suicide. *Journal of Abnormal Psychology,* 1966, 71, 389-399.

Seiden, R. *Suicide Among Youth. A Supplement to the Bulletin of Suicidology.* Washington: National Institute of Mental Health, 1969.

Schneidman, E.S. and Farberow, N.L. *Clues to Suicide.* N.Y.: McGraw Hill, 1957.

Some Frequent Questions
About Depression

Aren't there some physical causes of depression? Depression doesn't always come from anger does it?

Yes, there are physical causes of depression. A low thyroid condition, hypoglycemia, anemia, drug reactions, and other conditions can cause depression or can make an already existing depression worse. During adolescence, rapid body changes occur particularly in the endocrine system and can cause moodiness. Gifted children are not immune from physical problems, and these should, of course, be examined. Your child's feelings must still be handled sensitively.

Our 18 month old is already saying things to himself like "You're a bad boy" or "I'm sorry I'm so bad, Mommy." Is it really possible that he could really be aware of what he is saying?

He probably is quite aware of what he is saying, and what you are seeing is the development of his self-concept. It is important that he tell himself complimentary things as well as self-criticisms, and learn that he need not dwell on matters that are past. Assist him in seeing the difference between doing a "bad" or "dumb" thing, and being a "bad person." It may help if you ask him just how "bad" a person he feels he is, and what he thinks would make him a better person.

My daughter talks about committing suicide, and I have heard that gifted children are extremely likely to kill themselves. How do I know whether she is just trying to get attention or whether she is serious?

Please do not think that just because a child is gifted, she is virtually certain to commit suicide! Most gifted children grow up reasonably happy, content and feeling good about themselves — and we hope this book and others like it will help promote this. However, gifted children, as we have said, do seem more likely to experience depression, particularly if they have not been identified as gifted or have not received adequate support for their feelings and for their sense of self-worth. Children do sometimes think about suicide or say that they feel like killing themselves. Since this has happened with your daughter, you should remember two things. First, most people have suicidal thoughts at some time in their lives. Second, talk of suicide should always be listened to and considered seriously — not denied, ridiculed, challenged or ignored. Suicidal talk and gestures should be considered cries for help! Even when a suicidal gesture seems clearly an attempt to manipulate or punish someone, help is still needed to handle the angry, frustrated feelings underneath. Do not postpone getting professional help. Tell your child that you take her seriously, that you take her word for how unhappy she is, and that you know something must be done. Remind her that she should try every other possible alternative first — because once a person has committed suicide there are no alternatives left. Be alert for drug and alcohol use; persons who have been abusing such substances are more likely to commit suicide. Most of all, keep up your own courage, and get help for yourself if you need it, as well as for your child.

"No matter how many communes anybody invents, the family always creeps back."

Margaret Mead

"How many hopes and fears, how many ardent wishes and anxious apprehensions are twisted together in the threads that connect the parent with the child?"

Samuel Griswold Goodrich

"Taking care of their children, seeing them grow and develop into fine people, gives most parents — despite the hard work — their greatest satisfaction in life. This is creation. This is our visible immortality. Pride in our worldly accomplishments is usually weak in comparison."

Benjamin Spock

"Children are educated by what the grown-up is, not by his talk."

Carl Jung

"I love thee for a heart that's kind, not for the knowledge in thy mind."

W.H. Davies

"Intimates *trust* each other. They are not afraid that their partners exploit their weaknesses. They take turns at giving and taking but are not concerned with contract-like reciprocity. They tactfully respect each other's belt-lines, and temper their honesty with infinite tact so that a partner will not be cruelly hurt."

George Bach

"The family you come from isn't as important as the family you're going to have."

Ring Lardner

"Oh, to be only half as wonderful as my child thought I was when he was small, and only half as stupid as my teenager now thinks I am."

Rebecca Richards

CHAPTER XII

PARENT RELATIONSHIPS

Parenting gifted children puts you in a position that is different from most of your friends, neighbors and even relatives. Many friends and kin cannot empathetically relate to the rigors of raising an exceptionally bright child. Other adults may have difficulty understanding some of your attitudes and actions. For example, your child's advanced ability to handle various situations could enable you to allow unusual independence. You may feel that your nine year old can handle himself very well in your absence and is more responsible than the thirteen year old baby-sitter other parents may employ. Leaving him alone, however, could be interpreted by others as neglect.

Your concerns often will be different from the concerns of other parents, and they are likely to think that you are exaggerating when you describe your child's behaviors. Tensions with family and friends may well result. One parent told us that her mother-in-law called her "crazy" on learning that she allowed her ten year old daughter routinely to stay up until eleven o'clock at night. The child's mother was aware that gifted children often need less sleep; the grandmother was not. Although negative reactions sometimes reflect conscious jealousy, more often other adults simply have ideas, concerns and advice based on their own childhood experiences, "common knowledge," and observations of what can be expected from the average child. Educators may be particularly conditioned to have expectations based on what is true for the majority of children. Other professionals also often have inadequate understanding of the gifted child's growth, development, and impact on family and friends.

More than most parents, you may have to rely on yourself to determine what course is best for you and your child. You may need to grow away from some of the traditions with which you were raised. You may know what worked or did not work with you, but you need to question whether that style has the same effect on your gifted child. Other adults can be helpful only to a limited degree. Listen to their opinions, but develop the courage of your own convictions. You may have to develop the ability to stand fast against the prevailing winds.

Coming Out of the Closet

What was your reaction when you learned that your child is gifted? Did you tell everyone? Most parents tell only a few friends; others keep it a closely guarded family secret. Because of community attitudes, many parents feel they must keep the fact of giftedness in the closet. After one or two negative interactions with other parents, it is easy to decide to downplay a child's abilities.

Some of the difficulties stem from a semantic sensitivity to the term "gifted." In our country, where equal opportunity is a national goal, the implication that one person has been given special advantages by nature — "gifts" — leads people to complain of elitism. It is important for parents to remember that equal treatment and expectations for all, regardless of ability, is both unfair and unreasonable. In fact, our American ethic is based on the premise that the common person has the right to become uncommon according to his ability and his effort. Programs for the gifted are no more elitist than programs for athletes or for handicapped students. Our friends who care for mentally retarded, learning disabled, or physically handicapped children have become informed, sensitive and assertive; they have come out of the closet. It is probably necessary for parents of exceptionally gifted bright children to become advocates more openly.

Since the term "gifted" can create a distance from others, you may wish to use alternative phrases which describe your child without implying superiority. Practically speaking, other adults may accept your child's attributes less defensively if you say your child "concentrates intensely" or "loves to play with words," "is fascinated by mathematics," "always wants an explanation," "is extremely curious" or "loves to play with older children." If your child is exceptionally gifted, however, there may be no way of dealing with her differences without causing some sticky social situations. Just as the exceptionally gifted child has to learn to deal with other people's sometimes negative responses, you may have to accept a certain amount of misunderstanding from the world at large.

Household Harassment

If only there were enough hours in the day and the stamina to sustain us, parents might be able to accommodate everyone's expectations. One study (Kollstedt, 1981) estimated the average mother spends 99.6 hours in weekly household chores. As parenting roles have broadened, fathers also find themselves spending large amounts of time in family maintenance. It is difficult to keep a sense of balance among your sense of self, these chores and the demands of curious children who want you to share their current fascinations or concerns.

There are ways to reduce the time needed to attain acceptable levels of maintenance and to help take some of the hassle out of housework. You may need executive level training in management and efficiency skills through books (Bombeck, 1967; Lakein, 1974; Young & Jones, 1981) so that you will have more time to spend with your children. With gifted children, time is particularly of the essence, and will require your careful management.

What Is Your Image in the Home?

All parents want to bring fulfillment, competence, peace and enrichment into the lives of their children. But as we reflect on what we actually do and say, we discover that the image we present to our children is not necessarily the image we would choose. As Haim Ginott (1965) noted, "No parent wakes up in the morning planning to make his child's life miserable. No mother says to herself, 'Today I'll yell, nag, and humiliate my child whenever possible.' . . . yet in spite of good intentions . . . we find ourselves saying things we do not mean, in a tone we do not like."

Most often it is the many details of maintaining day-to-day life that lead us to feel overwhelmed and even resentful of our children's requests or demands. It may seem an overbearing imposition that you spend your life helping others with their priorities while your needs matter little.

You must take time to recharge you own batteries! You can only give what you have to give. Examine how you are investing in yourself. How do you include activities that make you more of the person you would like to be? Children need their parents not only to care for them and show an interest in their activities, but to provide an image of what people can be. Children need to see that their parents respect themselves as individuals and protect their rights to their *own* interests and activities as they protect those rights for the children. Once again it is a balancing act. You cannot give 100% of yourself to others; you cannot keep 100% of yourself for yourself.

Parenting Priorities

Each parent brings different parenting styles and attitudes about child-rearing into a marriage. Each has priorities, hopes, expectations and requirements for the children. Though they may be dimly aware of their own strongly held values when they marry, most people unrealistically expect marriage to create an instant fusion that will create a common parenting style. It does not happen. One young mother observed, "It seems that the ways my parents did things are right, but how my husband wants to raise our children is wrong."

In most families a shared parenting attitude emerges through trial and error, practice and many discussions. (Fortunately, children are too young to be aware of the first of these discussions when a couple faces the reality of parenthood in the early months.) As parents, you must sort out how much of your own ego and identity you are vicariously attributing to your child. You begin to recognize how many of your own hopes, fears and dreams lead you to over-react to your child's behaviors. The longer you are a parent, the more settled you become about what a good parent should be and what the right roles are for each parent.

Parenting Is Not Just "Mothering"

If a child knows both parents, despite separate living arrangements, both parents influence him. In the same way that he learns to speak a native language, a child will absorb attitudes, behaviors and expectations from his surroundings. It is widely recognized that a mother's warmth, support and interest influence a child's intelligence and creativity. Recent studies have shown that fathers significantly affect their child's intellectual development as well; excessive restrictiveness hinders intellectual ability, and nurturing and encouragement increases it (Radin, 1972; 1973; Sinn, 1978). Findings like these highlight the importance of attempting to develop shared parenting priorities and expectations.

The Single Parent

The divorce rate in the United States is rapidly approaching 40% and the number of single parents is growing. How does a parent manage the divorce situation with a gifted child? What can a single parent do to cultivate the greatest opportunity from this revised family situation? Questions like this have prompted whole books; but briefly, both divorce and single parenting require an added emphasis on communication when the children involved are gifted. Worries, guilt, depression and other feelings are particularly intense during this transition, both for you and for the child; and intimate special time becomes even more important.

The added pressures as a single parent combined with the apparent capability of the gifted child may lead you to depend heavily on him. Although this can deepen your relationship, you must be careful to avoid using your gifted child as a replacement for the absent parent. Your gifted child cannot be an adult confidante, nor can he assume parenting responsibilities for the other children. Highly intelligent children can intellectualize about situations, but you must remember that their emotional reactions are those of children.

In addition to the ideas given in this book, we refer you to publications such as *Marital Separation* (Weiss, 1975), *The Boys and Girls Book about Divorce* (Gardner, 1970), and *The Bookfinder* (1977). *The Bookfinder* deserves additional explanation. This unique book describes over 1,000 childrens' books, cross-referenced according to 450 topics of concern to children and young adolescents. It is available in libraries and is extremely valuable in helping guide gifted children's reading to specific areas of concern to them. Topics range from Abandonment to War.

Blended Families

Merging your styles of parenting is particularly difficult in blended families. In a blended family, both partners were parents in previous marriages and are now trying to blend two already established family styles into one. If this is your situation, *please* be patient with each other and yourself. Seldom can two separate and functioning parenting styles be mixed instantly in the on-the-job-training setting of raising children. Most parents grow up with their children, with years to coordinate their expectations about parenting and the life-style they wish to nurture.

Step-Parenting

As a step parent, how should you relate to your newly acquired step-child? We believe that each adult is responsible for establishing his own relationship with each child. This should be done with as much openness and sensitivity as the situation allows. Certainly, it helps if the step-parent understands many of the ways a gifted child is different from others and can accept those differences.

In blended families, one parent often tends to become the representative for his biological child. When a parent assumes that a child needs his protection, however, he discounts the child's competency and ability to be responsible for herself. Such a parent probably handicaps both the child and himself by not allowing her to establish her own relationship with the step-parent.

Life On the Front Lines

Sometimes one parent disagrees with the handling of a situation by the other parent. It is important to realize that many decisions are made on the front line and must be made quickly. Where one parent sets a limit, the other parent must reasonably avoid removing it, since gifted children are usually acutely aware of such divisiveness. For example, if Mom says, "Since you didn't eat your dinner, you may not have anything to eat until breakfast tomorrow," Dad should not later say, "Your mom was just upset. If you're really hungry, I'm sure it would be okay to get a snack." The only exception should be in cases where it appears that the child might suffer real physical or emotional damage unless you intervene. Usually, instead of undercutting your parent partner, you can request a huddle to check signals. Depending on the situation, you may be able to include the children. If the situation is especially difficult, parents can privately and quietly question a limit that has been set or is about to be set.

When a decision about discipline must be made, whichever parent or other adult is present must make it. It is not good practice to wait until the other parent gets home, or has had dinner and a drink. Not only will the delayed consequence lose its effectiveness from the time lag, but trust may be reduced. The child may feel more like the victim of a conspiracy than a person whose behavior has consequences.

Sometimes one parent protects the other parent from participation in situations that may be embarrassing to a child or parent. If can be tempting "not to worry Dad (or Mom) about it" and assume the burden alone. But this deceptive interception implies either that the child is not good enough for the other parent to accept, or that the other parent is not capable of handling matters appropriately. In either case, trust and acceptance may be hindered.

The House Rules

What are the best rules to establish? Beyond the basic principles outlined in this and similar books, there does not seem to be any golden set of house rules. Within these broad guidelines there clearly are many acceptable parenting styles that are largely a matter of taste, tradition and cultural heritage. The rules of each family are slightly different since they reflect the parents' values and character. Children, particularly gifted ones, quickly learn and adapt to house rules, usually without any great difficulty. They simply know that when they visit Grandma's house they do not use "that sort" of language, or when they visit their father and his new wife, they are expected to make their beds each morning. You generally do not need to fret that your house rules are not the same as the rules of some other place; your gifted child will likely adapt at least as quickly as you. In developing your house rules, base them on traits most valued by gifted children: honesty, responsibility and self-respect (Colangelo, 1976). Then your house rules can provide guidance that will flow with, rather than fight against, your children's strengths for emotional growth.

Summary

If we were to summarize our advice about parenting families with gifted children, we could not do better than to repeat *Desiderata* by Max Ehrman. So much that is contained in this work applies.

"Go placidly amid the noise and haste, and remember what peace there may be in silence. As far as possible without surrender, be on good terms with all persons. Speak your truth quietly and clearly; and listen to others, even the dull and ignorant; they too have their story.

Avoid loud and aggressive persons; they are vexations to the spirit. If you compare yourself there will be greater and lesser persons than yourself. Enjoy your achievements as well as your plans.

Keep interested in your own career, however humble; it is a real possession in the changing fortunes of time. Exercise caution in your business affairs; for the world is full of trickery. But let this not blind you to what virtue there is; many persons strive for high ideals; and everywhere life is full of heroism.

Be yourself. Especially do not feign affection. Neither be cynical about love; for in the face of all aridity and disenchantment it is perennial as the grass.

Take kindly the counsel of the years, gracefully surrendering the things of youth. Nurture strength of spirit to shield you in sudden misfortune. But do not distress yourself with imaginings. Many fears are born of fatigue and loneliness. Beyond a wholesome discipline, be gentle with yourself.

You are a child of the universe no less than the trees and the stars; you have a right to be here. And whether or not it is clear to you, no doubt the universe is unfolding as it should.

Therefore be at peace with God, whatever you conceive Him to be, and whatever your labors and aspirations, in the noisy confusion of life keep peace with your soul.

With all its sham, drudgery and broken dreams, it is still a beautiful world. Be cheerful. Strive to be happy."

215

References

Bach, G.B. and Wyden, P. *The Intimate Enemy: How to Fight Fair in Love and Marriage.* N.Y.: Avon, 1968.

Bach, G.R. and Deutsch, R.M. *Pairing: How to Achieve Genuine Intimacy.* N.Y.: Avon, 1970.

Bombeck, E. *At Wits End.* N.Y.: Doubleday, 1967.

The Bookfinder: A Guide to Children's Literature About the Needs and Problems of Youth Aged 2-15. Circle Pines, Minnesota: American Guidance Service, Inc., 1977.

Colangelo, N. and Zaffrann, R.T., *New Voices in Counseling the Gifted.* Dubuque, Iowa: Kendall/Hunt Publishing Company, 1979.

Gardner, R.A. *The Boys and Girls Book about Divorce.* N.Y.: Jason Aronson, 1970.

Ginott, H. *Between Parent and Child.* N.Y.: Avon Books, 1965.

Kollstedt, P.L. *Surviving the Crisis of Motherhood: Strategies for Caring for Your Child — and Yourself.* Cincinnati, OH: St. Anthony Messenger Press, 1981.

Lakein, A. *How to Get Control of Your Time and Your Life.* N.Y.: Signet, 1974.

Lewis, D. *How to Be a Gifted Parent.* N.Y.: Norton, 1981.

Perino, S.C. and Perino, J. *Parenting the Gifted.* N.Y.: Bowker Co., 1981.

Radin, N. Three degrees of maternal involvement in a preschool program: Impact on mothers and children. *Child Development,* 1972, 43, 1355-1364.

Radin, N. Observed paternal behaviors as antecedents of intellectual functioning in young boys. *Developmental Psychology,* 1973, 8, 369-376.

Shinn, M. Father absence and children's cognitive development. *Psychological Bulletin,* 1978, 85, 295-324.

Weiss, R.S. *Marital Separation.* N.Y.: Basic Books, 1975.

Young, P. and Jones, P. *Sidetracked Home Executives.* N.Y.: Warren Books, 1981.

Some Frequent Questions
About Parent Relationships

**Sometimes I feel I am being "bitten to death by ducks."
My gifted children need so much and are so demanding
that I feel there is nothing left of me to give. What can I do?**

It is insightful of you to recognize that you can only give what
you are. Your first responsibility needs to be caring for yourself
in some planned ways so that you don't burn out. You may wish
to use the family complaint department to discuss your concerns
and to insure that family members put into words the appreciation they feel for your efforts. You are the most important person
in a child's life, and need to remember that parenting is truly an
investment in a lifetime. If you invest wisely, the yields are
great. But this does not mean you must become a martyr who is
bitterly long-suffering and harbors a continual "low grade mad."
Use other adults in your family or community to enable you to
provide yourself some extra time. And remember that you are
the parent, and parents are in charge of families — not kids,
even if they are gifted.

**Sometimes I feel very inadequate to prepare my child for
what he is capable of doing. Do other parents feel that
way?**

Yes, they do. It may be an awesome responsibility to try to
keep pace with a gifted child. From infancy you are called upon
to be on duty 24 hours a day which includes trying to monitor
a childish, irresponsible, impulsive, verbose toddler who needs
less sleep than you do. Try to remember that Julia Child does
not do her work with a toddler or two on her lap. Eliminate the

non-essential tasks: homemade bread broken in bitterness is no better for *anyone* than sliced bread from the store. What is essential is your own satisfaction and inner equilibrium, and the emotional climate of your relationship. If you can supply courage, hope, and a healthy sense of self-worth to your child, just about everything else can wait.

How much should a parent be an advocate for a gifted child? When should she intervene in the school situation? I'm afraid that if I make suggestions to the teacher or point out some of the special needs of gifted children the teacher will take it out on my child.

If the child's health, safety or well-being are in jeopardy then you certainly need to intervene. We would suggest that you plan on a long-term project of helping to inform school personnel. Teachers, counselors, and school psychologists typically receive little, if any, training about gifted children and their families, and most of their education is "on the job." Even then, they probably have had little, if any, experience with exceptionally gifted children. They need your help. Join with other parents to establish an ongoing dialogue with principals, school boards, guidance counselors, teachers, and school psychologists. Obtain reading material for them; in-service training; invite speakers; establish affiliations with groups such as those listed in the last part of this book. When you talk with a teacher about a specific problem or situation, remember that you will have to start where the teacher is in his sophistication and knowledge about gifted children. Much of your first conference with a teacher will involve you learning about him and vice versa. It will also be necessary to remember some basics of communication: show understanding of his situation, particularly the emotional aspects; tell him what you are *not* saying, as well as what you are saying; check the communication by asking him to tell you what he hears you saying. If these guidelines are followed, teachers and parents usually find themselves working harmoniously together on a situation, with each feeling supported by the other. If such a relationship cannot be established with the teacher, however, feel free to go to the guidance counselor, or principal or other person in the school system who might be able to be a liaison or interpreter with the teacher. Unless the situation gets highly emotional it is not likely that the teacher will resent your concern and take it out on your child. If your child is exceptionally gifted, you must face the fact that you will need to be an advocate for him virtually all his school life. As Audrey Grost says, you may have to become a crusader! The above suggestions apply in dealing with educators, but you will need to be determined, constantly aware, and persistent. Keep firmly in mind that you know a great deal about your own child, and do not be discouraged.

Should parents tell their child he is gifted?

In some fashion or another you will have to confront the issue. He will recognize that he is different early in life, and he deserves an explanation. You do not have to use the word "gifted"; you can instead use words such as "quicker mentally" or "talented." Whatever words you use it is important to convey that giftedness is not an either/or thing — that is, others aren't "ungifted," but have different abilities. It is also important to convey that we all are interdependent and need to appreciate each person's special strengths.

Should I tell the aunts, uncles and grandparents that my daughter is gifted?

This depends on the relationship you have with these relatives and the relationship you have with your child. Whether she is gifted or not is basically between you and your child (and perhaps the school authorities). You may share this information with others if they will use it wisely. They should, however, appreciate the various cautions mentioned elsewhere in this book, and should avoid fostering a prima donna by publicly announcing to neighbors, store clerks, etc., "Well, you know that Mary is gifted!"

Should we get as much enrichment as possible for our child?

Basically the answer is yes, but with some cautions. Children are enriched by encouragement, participation and knowledge: areas of their own interest rather than in areas that vicariously gratify adults. One child should not become the primary focus of the family's activities, and you should not put so great a strain on the family budget that there are overt or covert resentments, or where the child feels burdened by excessively high expectations.

"The potential possibilities of any child are the most intriguing and stimulating in all creation."

Ray L. Wilbur

"Education commences at the mother's knee, and every word spoken within the hearsay of little children tends toward the formation of character."

Hosea Ballou

"Compared to what we ought to be, we are only half awake. We are making use of only a small part of our physical and mental resources."

William James

"Education is too important to be left to the educators."

Francis Keppel

"Education does not mean teaching people what they do not know. . . . It is a . . . continual and difficult work to be done with kindness, by watching, by warning, by precept and by praise, but above all — by example."

John Ruskin

"Education is a social process. . . . Education is growth. . . . Education is not a preparation for life; education is life itself."

John Dewey

CHAPTER XIII

AN OPEN LETTER TO PARENTS, TEACHERS AND OTHERS: FROM PARENTS OF AN EXCEPTIONALLY GIFTED CHILD

From Stephanie Tolan

In 1978 my husband and I officially learned that our son, RJ, is an exceptionally gifted child. He was tested two months before his sixth birthday, after we had done considerable research on giftedness and had met with numerous educators. As I write this, RJ is ten. The years in between have been full of ups and downs, of educational catastrophes and occasional periods of fairly smooth sailing. There are days when we find it hard to believe that our son is as different from the norm as the figures indicate, and other days when the difference is strikingly, blindingly obvious.

It took a long time for us to discover, and even longer to truly accept, that for children in the upper ranges of human intelligence the work being done to accommodate the educational needs of gifted children is simply *not enough*. Despite more than fifty years of research, the system has few answers to offer, so parents, teachers and children themselves continue to be pioneers.

For most purposes, I have found that children with IQ scores of 150+ are given the label "exceptionally" gifted, while a further grouping, sometimes called "profoundly" gifted, includes IQ scores of 180+. My own experience includes a child from each of these groups — my son and the son of my closest friend. Because our children are so different from the norm that even gifted programs don't meet their needs, because so few educators or other parents have had experience with children in these ranges, we find that one of our greatest problems is helping others to understand something of what we are dealing with. While it is hard for us to know what more normal children are like, it is very hard for others to know what our children are like or what they are capable of doing. Perhaps this open letter will provide some insights into life with an exceptionally gifted child.

Background

RJ was five years old before we began seriously to suspect that he was anything other than normally bright. The term "gifted" hadn't entered our normal vocabulary before then. This is true of most parents of gifted children. Their interest in giftedness is seldom a matter of choice.

If we had known when RJ was born what we know now, we would certainly have identified his capabilities by the time he was two. The symptoms would have been clear to anyone who knew how to interpret them; we didn't. Nor did anyone around us. Our three older boys, RJ's half-brothers, are all gifted, though we hadn't used that term for them as they were growing up in the 60's and early 70's, and we knew we had a bright family. Temperamentally, the older boys were quite different from each other, so as RJ grew, we attributed his differences to the fact that he was yet another individual. Certainly, he seemed to fit into the family well.

The other, probably the major, factor that kept us from realizing the extent of RJ's potential was that the son of my closest friend, born the same month as RJ, is also exceptionally — no, profoundly — gifted. (We know now that Jason's IQ, though it defies the Stanford-Binet test to some extent, is approximately 196.) Jason and RJ were raised almost together for the first three years of their lives, and did many of the same things at nearly the same time, though Jason was anywhere from a few weeks to six months ahead. Jason's mother and I did notice vast discrepancies between what our sons could do and what the Gesell Institute said they should be able to do at any given age, but we assumed that Gesell's guidelines were bare minimum, and we pretty well discounted them. We read, for instance, that a three to four year old should be capable of learning basic colors; because our 20 month old had already known them for some time, we simply gave up reading the book!

RJ first out-thought me when he was two and a half. We were taking an overnight train to visit my parents. After dinner he discovered the water fountain in the train car and was fascinated by the cone-shaped paper cups. He poured himself cup after cup, running up and down the aisle from the fountain to our seat with every cup. Finally, I told him he'd had enough, and put him into his pajamas. Then he asked for another drink. I told him that he couldn't go back to the fountain any more now that he was ready for bed. He began to fuss and I envisioned a "terrible two's" temper tantrum that would disturb everyone in the crowded coach and embarrass me, so I told him that there was no point in arguing with me — I was a grownup mother and he was a very little boy, and he could *never* win such a battle. "I will *always win!*" I said. (Now I see how thoroughly I deserved what I got.)

He abandoned his fussing and settled down to our usual routine of bedtime stories and a few wooden puzzles. Almost an hour passed in these activities, and then I told him it was time to go to sleep. At the time, he had to take a pill before bed each night, and he usually swallowed the pill with water. He offered to get the water for taking his pill. Without thinking, I set him in the aisle and he padded off for the water. When he'd returned with it and had taken his pill, he smiled angelically and said, "You see, Mom, I *did* win!" I remember quite clearly wondering what I would do with this child when he got to be 13. Since then, I've learned that he thrives on the kind of challenge situation I had unwittingly set up.

Very early in RJ's life he was noticed and his conversations were commented upon in grocery stores, restaurants and other public places. Being used to his conversations and not knowing how other small children talked, I assumed he was being noticed because he was a cute little boy. Later, when he began to read, it became clear that it was not his appearance drawing attention. People would ask how old he was and then, to our discomfort, tell us — over his head — how "smart" he was. We began to notice a tendency on his part to "play to an audience." His natural and fairly sophisticated sense of humor got him plenty of laughs whenever he wanted them. We didn't know then that his sense of humor was typical of highly gifted children, so we thought of him not as "smart," but as "theatrical," and rather show-offy.

We also learned early that he was highly creative, but we didn't know that creativity was ever likely to be accompanied by exceptional intellectual gifts. He was exceedingly sensitive to the emotions of other people, highly empathetic, and very loving and cuddly. These were not attributes we associated with brilliance either. What we were most aware of during his early years was that he was a great deal of fun to be with. He was two and a half when he first said what I recognized as a "poem." He had asked about why the leaves were falling and being raked up, so I'd tried to explain autumn to him. He thought very seriously for a moment and then said, "The leaves will fall off the tree and they will cry. They will say, 'Mommy, Mommy, we are green and yellow and sad!'" Because I was a poet, I supposed that I was

unusually attuned to what poetry there might be in the ut-
terances of two year olds, and thought his "poem" probably
expressed a typical two year old view of the world in which
trees and leaves might talk and separation from mother was the
ultimate sadness. I did not know many two year olds.

Highly gifted children are individuals, just as other children
are. Their personalities, temperaments, likes and dislikes are
as varied as in any other group. Temperamental differences may
also account for the failure of parents to recognize extreme
giftedness early. We believed the myth that all "genius" children
are unhappy or very solitary or seriously maladjusted, and RJ
had been from birth a happy, outgoing, warm and generally
contented person. As a baby he cried only to let us know when
he was hungry or in pain. By six months he was contented with
sitting in his car-bed for literally hours at a time, quietly looking
at his toys, sometimes sucking on them contemplatively. Even
as an infant he was already what he was to be labeled in school
— "a dreamer." He was always extremely observant and seldom
apparently either bored or frustrated. Throughout his infancy he
met new people and new situations easily and apparently without fear.

Jason was as different, it seemed, as was possible for a baby
to be. He cried often and long and seemed never to be content
with anyone or anything. He wanted always to be moving.
While RJ was sitting at 6 months, Jason was doing his frustrated
best to crawl, shrieking in fury when he couldn't manage it. He,
too, was extremely observant, but demanded a constant change
in stimuli. It was almost as if Jason felt a prisoner in that unco-
ordinated body, almost as if he were at war with himself. Like
RJ, however, he never seemed to be afraid of new people or new
situations, and found anything new worth investigating.

Today they are still very different children. Jason still demands constant stimulation — books to read, projects to work

on, materials for arts and crafts or building. RJ is still a dreamer who engages in projects, but who also spends long periods of time entertaining himself inside his own mind. Their interests are not the same, but they are able to share them with each other, and despite their temperamental differences, they are still happier with each other than either has been with another child.

Many people who know RJ have told me that any other highly gifted children they have known have been unhappy children. They've suggested that Bob and I must be doing something right as parents that would account for RJ's obvious happiness. It might be comforting — it's certainly tempting — to believe that it has been our parenting that has made our son happy, but that would be neither true nor fair to parents of the unhappy ones. RJ has been cheerful and sunny since the beginning. His basic temperament is as much a part of him as his hair color.

What accounts for the observation that most exceptionally gifted children are unhappy? It is apparently not a mistaken observation — research shows that while the 130-140 range gifted child is likely to be unusually stable, happy, competent and outwardly successful, the 150+ child is likely to have emotional problems ranging from minor to severe. Have they all been born to "bad" parents or unstable families? Obviously, the answer can't lie in the family alone. These children are forced to live in a society for which they aren't suited. They don't "fit" their culture. They don't fit the expectations of others. In particular, they don't fit school, usually a rigid environment in which they spend a large portion of their waking hours.

A further complication is that these are the very children who ought to fit best in an educational environment. School seems to hold out for them the greatest promise. Their special joy in life is learning, so they are the children who expect the greatest rewards and joys in school. When the reality of school life turns out to be manifestly negative — holding them back rather than helping them move ahead — they must deal not only with that negativity, but with the shattering of their high expectations. The child who dreads school may only nod cynically if it turns out to be bad. The child who has looked forward to school as the fulfillment of his dreams is disappointed almost beyond bearing when it falls so desperately, incomprehensibly short. Even the child blessed with a naturally easy-going disposition cannot survive year after year of a school's apparent refusal to let him learn without serious emotional damage.

It is also unfair to lay all the blame on the schools. Highly gifted children are difficult children to raise, no matter what their temperament. The example of RJ in the train stands out only because it was the first most obvious example of his having outwitted me. Similar events take place regularly. It can be almost unbelievably difficult for a parent to be subjected to the constant scrutiny of a child who, whether two or twelve, takes intense delight in pointing out inconsistencies, discovering errors and exposing clay feet. No parent can think out every response to a child before opening his or her mouth!

In addition, the highly gifted child requires an *enormous* investment of time, energy and money from his parents. As a psychologist pointed out in a speech to a parent group, it takes the cost of a Mercedes Benz to raise a child today, and the cost of two to raise a gifted child. Most people understand that having a handicapped child is a severe strain on a family. Few understand that the same is true with an exceptionally gifted child. As the psychologist further pointed out, the parents never bargained for the position, so almost certainly resent the extreme demands at least part of the time.

Finally, there are the complications of ego involvement for parents. The gifted child has an almost uncanny ability to sense when a parent is "using" the child's abilities to boost his or her own ego. We'd like to think this never happens, but we'd be fooling ourselves. When he was small, RJ's method of fighting back when he felt used was to talk baby talk, particularly in public. Because the children are quicker to sense our need for them to appear gifted than we may be, I found the frequency with which he resorted to the baby talk weapon particularly depressing. It takes very little reasoning to see that his baby talk made me uncomfortable in direct proportion to how much I was depending on him to prove his giftedness.

When you consider the strains a parent must deal with, then add the complications encountered when the child is not only highly gifted but also temperamentally difficult, it is possible to understand why some parents appear not to deal very well with their very bright children, and why the parents need special help.

School

Until the exceptionally gifted child goes to school, there may be few, if any, serious difficulties with him. Often, as in RJ's case and Jason's case, the child is not identified before beginning regular school. At home and in some good, open nursery schools, there may be enough flexibility to allow the child to be himself, regardless of how different that is from the norm. Eventually, however, the child is sent to school and, one way or another, the trauma begins. Reactions to school may be different, but the one thing that seems inevitable is that in school obstacles are placed in the way of learning, usually for the first time. Children react in one or more negative ways, though some of those ways are not recognized at first as negative. Some children attempt to please adults by rigidly adhering to the system's requirements, some withdraw, other rebel and become disruptive. Some try each of these responses in turn. But in every case there is real damage to their attitudes, learning patterns and abilities.

Having begun five-mornings-a-week preschool at 28 months, RJ had already had three years of serious but open-ended education when he began full day kindergarten at a public Montessori school. He could not understand why no one gave him anything to read and why there was nothing to do in this new school except "play." When I spoke to his teacher about arranging for some reading, she explained that RJ was being very patient with them, but that with 28 other children, many of whom knew no numbers, no letters and few colors, she and her assistant could not do much for RJ. As soon as she could, she got him into a group with others in his class who could read, though for the whole year he remained unchallenged and felt he was not learning anything. However, he enjoyed recess, lunch, art and music well enough to stay reasonably happy and didn't complain too much. For the first time school had become a place to endure instead of an environment in which he was free to explore and learn at his own pace.

Because he did endure it, we didn't suspect the magnitude of his problem until I did a poetry residency at his school with third, fourth and fifth graders. I had never worked with such young children before and I understood immediately that something was very wrong. Either his school was such a dreadful school that middle grade children knew very little more than kindergarten children, or RJ was not at all a normal kindergarten child. The chief difference I noted between working with those students and dealing with RJ was that I had to stop more often to explain the words I used to the older children than I did with RJ. He seemed able to do anything they could do, except that they were learning to write cursive, while he could only print. So began our voyage of discovery.

I began to read a little and wondered if our son could possibly be "gifted." We began to write down examples of our interactions with him that showed the way he thought and learned.

One of these occurred one day when he was home sick from kindergarten. He asked me to tell him what 45 times 18 was. I figured it out and told him, then asked why he wanted to know (since he'd only had adding and subtracting under 10 in school, I didn't know he even knew what multiplication was). He said there were too many holes in the top of his aquarium to count them all, so he'd only counted one long side and one short side, but the numbers were too big for him to multiply. We still have no idea how he understood that principle. We only know he had never been taught.

As these examples grew into a small portfolio, we decided that the next step was to take them to "experts" and find out whether RJ was unusually bright. That is when we had our first encounter with what virtually all parents of gifted children must contend with throughout the children's school years — the denial syndrome. Even *taking* our suspicions to eductors was embarrassing and a little frightening. What if we were wrong? What if we were overestimating, showing ourselves to be typical doting parents?

That is exactly what we *were* told! Our motives, our observations, our honesty and finally our parenting methods were questioned. We were told that while RJ's accomplishments might be *somewhat* unusual, they were far from amazing and could probably be accounted for by our having pushed him ahead too fast, started him in school too early, demanded too much from him. We were led to believe that given our terrible pressure on him, he was lucky to be as yet fairly normal. Most of all, we were assured that he could be handled by his school, in which there were *many* equally bright children, being educated quite well!

His teacher, when we took these assessments to her, strongly disagreed. She knew that far from pushing, an adult usually had to work to keep up with RJ. She told us she had never known a student as bright as he and warned that finding him an education that would suit his capabilities would be hard, and would involve a battle with the schools. She advised us to have him tested so we could go into that battle armed with numbers that would command respect. And so we had reached the next step; we arranged with a private psychologist to have RJ tested.

Testing

I'll never forget driving home after the first of three testing sessions, certain that we were stark, staring mad, that his tests were going to prove he was exactly what we had always thought him to be — a bright normal child. It may be hard for other people to understand the emotional upheaval parents go through when they begin the testing procedure. We believed that brilliant people were seriously maladjusted and that everyone would be better off somewhere in the comfortable middle. The fact that RJ was so happy seemed to mean either that he wasn't gifted or that he would soon become unhappy and weird. Though we hoped the testing would show he was gifted, at the same time we were afraid that it might. We saw that our egos were involved and wondered if the tests showed him to be "normal" if we would be seriously disappointed, and perhaps make him feel he had somehow failed us.

On the other hand, if he did turn out to be gifted, would we begin pressuring him in destructive ways? Could we, in fact, handle what we were going to learn about our son? We had no way of knowing. Was intellectual precocity a good thing to have anyway? Clearly, the answer to that one didn't matter. RJ was who he was, and all we were doing was trying to learn enough about him to help him and ourselves cope with that reality.

Since then, I've talked to a number of parents of highly gifted children, and all of them tell of these emotional ups and downs about testing. In addition to all those questions, most of us had already made a rather considerable fuss about a proper education, and we were risking a great deal of embarrassment if we were proven wrong. While those may be unworthy concerns, they're quite real.

The other memorable moments were when the psychologist told me, after her last session with him, but before she'd worked out the numbers, that RJ was the brightest child she'd ever tested — a moment for me, of stark terror — and the drive home after Bob's and my final meeting with her, when we faced together the fact that RJ actually belonged in the range that is sometimes referred to as "genius." Though we were pleased to be vindicated after our unpleasant encounters with educators, we were afraid of what we faced in finding him an education, and of what he faced in finding a place for himself in the world.

Jason's parents, too, decided to have Jason tested, taking him to a school psychologist. They were told that Jason's IQ was 150. This score would have put him below RJ, and made no sense to me at all. No one explained to them that the test they'd used had a ceiling of 150. No one suggested that further testing might be more accurate. When his mother and I tested his reading and discovered that he was reading 800 words per minute with almost total comprehension the summer he was six, we began to suspect that the test had not told the whole story. In my reading, I found that children with IQ's over 180 are very likely to teach themselves to speed read, so we guessed that he might actually belong in that category. Even so, none of us really knew what that meant or *how* different either of the boys might be from other children their age. Jason and RJ were both expected somehow to "fit in" at school, perhaps with a little extra help and input from their parents.

Research

As I began looking for a school willing to make a commitment to educating RJ, I began the research into the subject of gifted education that continues to be part of my life today. I really thought, then, that all I had to do was read widely enough and I would find the answers. It took many months before I could admit that there didn't seem to be any answers, or else that there were many, many answers that contradicted each other. More than fifty years ago Leta Hollingworth pointed out that 150+ children could learn all of the standard elementary school material in one fourth the normal time — or less. But since then, no one has offered a way to let them routinely do that. She said that these children "waste" at least three fourths of their time in the classroom and that the 180+ children waste nearly all of it. But where were the suggestions about how to avoid such a waste? And who could tell us how to help our children cope with a system that ate up six hours a day when even on weekends or summer vacations they always had more to do than there was time for? How could we justify to them the loss of all those hours?

It's hard for parents to give up the belief that schools should know how to educate their highly gifted child. And it's equally hard for teachers to believe what parents say about the ways these children learn. It's hard for anyone to believe what they can do, even when you see it, because it can seem almost supernatural. As one person said, it is almost as if they don't have to learn anything, needing only to be reminded of it. What the research and our day-to-day experience proves most clearly is that highly gifted children cannot fit into most existing educational systems. So the stage is set for difficult and often unpleasant confrontations between parents and educators.

The story of Edison, who was declared unfit for education, is not an unusual one. The highly gifted child learns in ways that are very different from the ways schools teach. While most educational methods present one small step at a time, one detail, to which another and then another are added in a specific progression until the larger picture can be seen, the gifted child makes a "giant leap" and sees the overall picture almost immediately. When he is then required to concentrate on the details — often for weeks at a time — he finds it difficult, boring and apparently purposeless.

Putting the highly gifted child into a normal classroom may be likened to putting a natural runner at the beginning of a running track on which every step is carefully painted and numbered. He is told to run the track, putting his feet into each proper space in turn. When he tries to run that way, he stumbles, falters and loses his natural rhythm, balance and stride. But if he gives up the attempt and runs in the way that is most natural to him, anyone evaluating him on how well he puts his feet into the proper painted spaces would consider him a dismal failure. Either way, it looks as if he is not very good at what he is supposed to do.

Parents continually have to deal with educators who are doing exactly that — evaluating the child on how well he puts his feet into those spaces. And so we are told that our children are *not* as bright as we think they are. We are told that, in fact, there are several other children in the shool or in his class, who are much brighter. Or we may be told that if he really *is* bright, he is clearly stubborn, antisocial and difficult to handle. Most educators don't understand the difference between extreme intellectual ability and "academic talent" that succeeds well within the system. It is a help at such times to remember that Einstein was considered dull and slow, that Edison was "unfit," and that Picasso was "strange."

Parents find themselves in confrontation with educators primarily because parents are the first to notice that the experience of school may be doing serious emotional damage. Parents know what the child was like before he went to school and see the personality changes caused by frustrating the child's innate desire to learn and by attempting to force the child into a pattern that doesn't fit him. But even parents often take longer than they should, partly because they look for other explanations first, and partly because they don't want to admit that schooling is the cause, knowing there may be very little they can do to change the school situation.

RJ and Private School

On our psychologist's advice, after visiting many schools, we decided on a private school whose Individually Guided Education program seemed to provide some flexibility. RJ began first grade and we decided to stay out of the way, letting this expensive good school do its work. We didn't want to interfere partly because we didn't think we knew much about educating first graders and partly because I had no desire to be the mother everybody would run from. (I didn't know it was a role I would have to learn to live with.) We had provided the school with test scores, a full psychological evaluation, and as much explanation as we could give them on the way RJ learned, and assumed they would use that information appropriately. By the first parent-conference in November, RJ had reached the point of feigning illness in the morning to avoid going to school. Having already "wasted" a year in kindergarten, he had run out of patience.

With the support of the psychologist we made some changes at that time — giving him a fifth grade reader and a fifth grade vocabulary book, for instance — that seemed to help. But again, if I had known then what I know now, I would have recognized sooner that we had changed nowhere nearly enough. By the spring RJ was no longer a warm, outgoing, happy child. He had become grumpy, difficult, argumentative and prone to temper tantrums. Our interactions at home became more and more negative until we were fighting almost all the time. First we blamed ourselves — we must be doing something wrong with him suddenly — then we decided it must be a developmental phase that had something to do with turning seven. We were forgetting that we had weathered all the typical developmental hot spots with RJ quite easily. Nothing had prepared us for the possibility that school could be responsible for such sweeping changes.

Luckily, though we hadn't focused in on school problems, we did see that RJ was having difficulty relating to chronological peers. Though he would agree to play games his classmates wanted to play, he complained that they would never play the games he wanted to play. He had difficulty placing himself with them, difficulty knowing who he was supposed to be. He didn't understand their preferences; they didn't understand his. He began imitating some of their wilder behavior in his attempt to belong, and was confused when that behavior caused particular trouble for him with adults who had learned to expect him to be more controlled. We insisted that he be moved from Unit I (grades one and two) to Unit II (grades three and four) for the following year. I knew that Unit II children were treated less like babies than Unit I children, and we hoped that higher expectations would be better for him. He has *never* liked to be "treated like a child."

When school was over at the end of the first grade year, it was as if someone had pushed a magic button. The RJ we knew was suddenly back! Gone were the grumps, the temper tantrums, the constant conflict. We finally understood that the culprit *was* school — educationally, socially, in every way. Free to choose companions from an age range unlimited by grade level, he was able to interact happily with children younger than he, his age, older, and — as always — clearly enjoyed being with adults. As is common with children whose mental age and chronological age are very different, he chose his most constant companions from mental rather than chronological peers, but continued to prefer the combination. He and Jason, though by this time living in different states, enjoyed their visits with each other enormously, freely ranging from the talk and behavior of twelve year olds down to seven — or lower — and back up again.

Jason's first grade year had been survivable because he had a teacher who allowed him to finish work as quickly as possible and take refuge in reading. He had less trouble with classmates than RJ because he avoided interacting with them whenever he could. None of us knew that while allowing Jason to read did keep the peace and fill his time, it would strengthen his already growing tendency to shut out the difficult and often inexplicable outside world and retreat to the safety of books. The ground was being prepared for withdrawal.

Our school had put up a fight over acceleration and predicted dire consequences if we actually put RJ into third grade. "It has *never* worked!" we were told. By this time, we had begun to trust our own assessments, however, and once again we were vindicated. After a couple of weeks in a third/fourth grade classroom, he joined a group of gifted fourth graders in language arts and by the end of the year had completed fourth grade with ease. His biggest difficulty had to do with the amount of paper work required of fourth graders. He loathed doing homework after six hours of school; his handwriting — so newly learned — was no match in speed or legibility for that of his classmates, and though he learned to type, he could not do everything on a typewriter. In addition, his naturally dreamy and scattered approach to life caused difficulty with organization. Socially, he had great success, getting along far better with fourth graders than he ever had with children his own age. Perhaps the most important factors in his success were his two teachers, kind and caring people who wanted him to make it and were willing to make an effort to understand the way he learned.

Meanwhile, Jason — in second grade in public school — had met his Waterloo. His new teacher didn't allow him to read when he finished his work, and tried hard to "help" him fit in with the other children. After only a couple of months, he had reached a point of such confusion and pain that his withdrawal became absolute. He would speak to no person, child or adult, from the moment he set foot inside the school building until he left. At home he clearly showed his rage at his parents for continuing to send him off to what he considered torture five days a week. It was then that his parents found a psychologist to test him (using a Stanford-Binet this time) and started therapy for him. It can be said fairly accurately that only twice-a-week therapy got Jason through the second grade without serious and possibly permanent damage.

RJ's second year of acceleration worked far less well than the first, in spite of the fact that the group of children he had moved up with remained supportive and friendly. He was now in Unit III, with new teachers — an eight year old in class with both fifth and sixth graders. The sixth graders gave him a steady diet of teasing and his new teacher not only failed to support him, but subtly undermined his position, frequently reminding everyone that he was both younger and smaller. Her comments on his end-of-the-year report card, in spite of his good grades, were a summary of a year in which he had been criticized for being "immature" and "disorganized," and told over and over that his study habits were poor. Again, it had been a year in which homework had caused friction at home. His school put a premium on "homework as discipline" and RJ did not think he should have to do work that had no purpose except to take his time. He greeted the end of the year with joy and relief.

Jason had had a far better year, even though he had been kept with other eight year olds in the third grade. He had been moved to a private school that had agreed to try to make a supportive environment for him, and he found another gifted child who became a friend. Continued therapy helped as well, and by spring he and his family felt that things were going well enough that they could drop regular therapy.

During the summer after RJ's fifth grade year, we moved to another state, and a hasty school search had to be undertaken. I had learned something by then that I think is vital in trying to find a place for the exceptionally gifted child. Private academic schools that pride themselves on sending students on to ivy league colleges, that publish honor rolls and class standings, may not be appropriate for exceptionally gifted children. Such schools may be very good for many gifted children, especially left-brained achievers, but the chief characteristic of the most highly gifted is not only their ability to learn, but the difference in their methods of learning. One must be careful to avoid schools whose procedures and patterns are too rigid to allow for those differences. Heavy competition for grades and public achievement may not be as important to the exceptionally gifted child as his need to explore whatever subjects he wants to explore. The social pressure common in that environment is especially hard on the highly gifted child who is, by definition, very different. Finally, the academic school is likely to be especially defensive about its reputation for handling "the best and the brightest." They may be particularly unwilling to consider the possiblity that any child needs something they don't offer.

We were lucky enough to find a private school that is extremely flexible, designed to allow each child to progress at his or her own rate. In an environment where every child is seen as an individual, RJ is no more noticeably an individual than the others. While an especially caring teacher was once again responsible for the success of RJ's year, the school's philosophy of nonviolence and tolerance for differences provided the background for good social interaction. As for academic growth, the result was more mixed. Technically, he was called a fifth grader again, though his work was from standardly junior high texts, and he probably didn't learn what he is capable of learning. However, he was comfortable, he liked the approach the school takes to learning, and he had a chance to try new things — drama, pottery and running. His comfort in school means a great deal, because it allows him to be himself at home and to pursue his out-of-school interests with the energy and enthusiasm lacking in uncomfortable years.

The year was once again disastrous for Jason, who was still kept with chronological peers in fourth grade. Social interactions became more and more difficult, finally violent; there was nothing for him to learn in the classroom; his teacher lost no opportunity to accentuate his difference by trying to force him to interact with the others. Jason asked to resume therapy, and his parents have decided that next year they will try a new tack, in a new school, with whatever combination of radical subject-matter acceleration and out-of-school learning they can arrange. It has taken a long time to be finally convinced that an over 180 child is so different that minor alterations of normal school methods can't be enough.

There are frustrations to living with an exceptionally gifted child that can get parents down. It can mean living in a perpetually messy world of half-completed projects and discarded socks. It can mean continual conferences, often emotional and usually frustrating, with educators. It can mean demands on time and resources that seem unreasonable and somehow unfair. It can mean — regularly — sending a child to brush his teeth and finding him an hour later, teeth unbrushed, deeply involved in perfecting a new paper airplane, making a dragon out of clay or building a skyscraper out of drinking straws.

But there are many compensations. I can't imagine a parent, even in the midst of the greatest traumas, who would really want to trade such a child in on another model. We have been given a gift as well — a unique child to be loved and cared for and enjoyed as we try to find ways to help him reach his potential.

There are no cookbooks, no guidelines, no educational courses that provide *sure-fire* methods of parenting and educating the highly gifted child. We are all pioneers, and will need to share our resources and information with each other. When he was four, RJ was told by another child in his nursery school car pool that he would not be invited to that child's birthday party. RJ looked at him for a moment and then said, "You don't exist. You are only in my mind." We don't know very much about that mind, except that it would be criminal to tie it down.

"The man who does not read good books has no advantage over the man who can't read them."

Mark Twain

"The books that help you the most are those which make you think the most."

Theodore Parker

"To read without reflecting is like eating without digesting."

Edmund Burke

"These are not books, lumps of lifeless paper, but *minds* alive on the shelves."

Gilbert Highet

"Acquire new knowledge whilst thinking over the old, and you may become a teacher of others."

Confucius

CHAPTER XIV

ANNOTATED BIBLIOGRAPHY

A. Journals and Periodicals

- *Gifted Child Quarterly,* Gifted Education Resource Institute, Purdue University, SCC-G, West Lafayette, IN 47907. This scholarly journal contains articles on pilot programs, demonstration projects and giftedness research. It is primarily for teachers, researchers and well informed parents.

- *Journal for the Education of the Gifted,* The Association for the Gifted, Council for Exceptional Children, 1920 Association Dr., Reston, VA 22091. A scholarly journal focusing on research and education, this publication would be helpful to teachers, researchers and enlightened parents of gifted children.

- *G/C/T (Gifted/Creative/Talented),* Box 66654, Mobile, AL 36660. This bimonthly journal emphasizes articles on identifying and educating the creative and gifted, though it also contains other items of interest to parents and teachers of gifted and creative. The activity ideas and insights are quite helpful to a broad range of readers.

- *Journal of Creative Behavior,* Creative Education Foundation Inc., State University College at Buffalo, 1300 Elmwood Ave., Buffalo, NY 14222. A broad range of articles is included focusing on research in creativity, creative problem solving, and creative educational methods. It is for parents and teachers.

- *The Creative Child and Adult Quarterly,* National Association for Creative Children and Adults, 8080 Spring Valley Dr., Cincinnati, OH 45236. This is a research and education-oriented journal on creative and gifted persons. Both teachers and parents will find it enlightening.
- *Gifted Children Monthly,* P.O. Box 115, Sewell, NY 08080. This newsletter is primarily for parents, but it includes activities for children. Brief reports of programs and research are written in laymen's language, along with information about conferences, meetings and reviews of books. This publication is a valuable resource.
- *National/State Leadership Training Institute on the Gifted and Talented Bulletin,* National/State Leadership Training on the Gifted and Talented, Ventura County, 316 West Second St., Suite PH-C, Los Angeles, CA 90012. This bulletin brings news of workshops, research, parent involvement, resource materials and more. It is mostly for parents and teachers, and is written in easy to read style.
- *The Roeper Review,* 2190 N. Woodward, Bloomfield Hills, MI 48013. A quarterly journal with a broad focus, this publication presents academic, philosophical and moral issues of gifted children. The contents are scholarly, and often require some expertise in psychology or education. The book reviews are well done and worthwhile.

B. Books, Articles and Other Resources
- Alvino, James, and the editors of *Gifted Children Monthly, Parents' Guide to Raising a Gifted Child.* Boston: Little, Brown and Company, 1985. This wide-ranging, practical resource of parenting advice and troubleshooting techniques is compiled by experts and experienced parents. Topics are extensive and include identification of bilingual, L.D., and minority children, effective parent advocacy, preschool, under-

achievement, depression and suicide, and coping with high expectations.

- American Association for Gifted Children, *On Being Gifted*. NY: Walker and Co., 1978. This book is an excellent resource for parents, and helpful for gifted kids, themselves. Twenty gifted teenagers have written about themselves and their giftedness. Their descriptions provide perspective and insight. These successful and talented young persons edited the book, and published it through the AAGC. There is no substitute for reading what gifted children say about gifted children.
- Anthony, J.B. and Anthony, M.M., *The Gifted and Talented, A Bibliography and Resource Guide*. Pittsfield, MA: Berkshire Community Press, 1981. A resource for those who want to do research or to study further, this book contains over 3,000 references. It constitutes an update on Laubenfels's annotated bibliography published in 1977.
- Barbe, Walter B. and Renzulli, Jospeh, (Eds.), *Psychology and Education of the Gifted*. NY: Irvington Publishers, 1975. This anthology represents some of the most significant contributions for understanding and developing gifted children. The many authors, including Hollingsworth, Gallagher and Terman, provide an overview of research in the field. These findings relate to the needs and characteristics of gifted children and include alternatives to stimulate their strengths.
- Blakeslee, Thomas R., *The Right Brain: A New Understanding of the Unconscious Mind and Its Creative Powers*. New York: Anchor Press, 1980. An excellent introduction to the research on hemisphericity.
- Branden, Dr. Nathaniel, "Dealing With the Gifted Child," Jeffrey Norton Publishers, Inc., 145 East 49th Street, New York, NY 10017. This audio cassette tape available at many libraries provides enlightenment for practically no time investment! Here are provocative perspectives and questions that seldom surface

about gifted children such as: What are the factors that obstruct human ability from actualizing itself? Why does the gifted child embark on a systematic effort to cut herself down to acceptable size? It demonstrates how people express subtle sarcasm, turnoffs and putdowns that penalize kids for being outgoing about their intelligence. Do we really respect novelty, or do we unconsciously make our payoffs conditional on the child's performing as we think he should?

- Bricklin, Barry and Bricklin, Patricia M., *Bright Child — Poor Grades, The Psychology of Underachievement.* NY: Delacorte Press, 1967. To achieve understanding and empathy, the multiple psychological causes of underachievement are extensively examined. Then, recommendations for attitudes and action to infuse encouragement and positive motivation are offered. The Bricklins have gone beyond games and gimmicks to provide an insightful resource for parents and teachers to cooperatively help a gifted child's strengths work for him.

- Briggs, Dorothy Corkille, *Your Child's Self-Esteem.* Garden City, NY: Doubleday and Co., 1970. How a child will relate to his world is based on his self-esteem. This book provides techniques and concepts that may enable you to convey that your child is capable, worthwhile and lovable. It explores specific situations and areas of concern with behavior examples indicating means to nurture cooperation and positive feelings.

- Clark, Barbara, *Growing Up Gifted.* Columbus, OH 43216: Charles E. Merrill Publishing Company, 1979. This comprehensive resource contains extensively researched data integrated with sensitive understanding to provide enrichment. School settings, strategies for teaching and various specific areas of concern in gifted education are discussed, in addition to some new frontiers in brain research and other areas.

- Colangelo, N., and Zaffran, R.T. (Eds.), *New Voices in Counseling the Gifted.* Dubuque, IA: Kendall/Hunt, 1979. This extensive compilation of research examines gifted children, their families, schools and careers. Implications from articles provide foundations for developing principles and practices of understanding, stimulating and guiding gifted children. Topics include counseling the culturally diverse gifted, the handicapped gifted, career and lifestyle determinants in gifted women, and values of gifted students and their parents.

- Coleman, Daniel, "1,528 Little Geniuses and How They Grew," *Psychology Today*, February, 1980. This article highlights a 56-year follow-up perspective on what made a difference in the lives, patterns, and satisfactions of the Terman study children. It reveals many persuasive points such as that a sense of competence was tremendously important for gifted women, and that happy children grew up to be happy adults!
- Comer, James P. and Poussaint, Alvin J., *Black Child Care*. NY: Pocket Books/Simon and Schuster, 1975. Written by two black Yale University psychiatrists, this book should be read by anyone parenting, teaching or working with black children. Practical comments and advice abound, and the book provides important understanding of the black experience of child-rearing.
- Cox, June, *Educating Able Learners: Programs and Promising Practices*. Austin, TX: University of Texas Press, 1985. Based on a national study conducted by the Sid W. Richardson Foundation, this book provides a current and poignant overview of our nation's attempt to educate our most able learners (a somewhat broader category than "gifted") based on such diverse sources as Macarthur Fellows and school surveys. This book will continue to impact gifted education for some time, and is important reading regarding current practices and future directions.
- Dabrowski, K. and Piechowski, M.M., *Theory of Levels of Emotional Development, Vols. I and II*. Oceanside, NY: Dabor

Science Publishing, 1977. Dabrowski's theory of emotional and moral development, an important addition to Maslow and Kohlberg, is also among the more exciting concepts in explaining both the differences between gifted individuals and others, and differences among gifted. A clear introduction to this material can be found in M.M. Piechowski's article, "The Concept of Developmental Potential," *Roeper Review,* (Vol. 8, No. 3, Feb., 1986).

- Delisle, James R., *Gifted Children Speak Out.* New York: Walker and Co., 1984. Over 6,000 gifted children answered questionnaires to create this analysis of how they feel and manage being gifted. Responses are categorized into areas such as future goals, defining giftedness, school, and getting along with friends. The corresponding sections of discussion guides and classroom activities complement the children's responses to stimulate insight, empathy, and constructive self management.

- *Directory for Exceptional Children: A Listing of Educational and Training Facilities,* 8th Edition, 11 Beacon Street, Boston, MA 02108: Porter Sargent Publishers, Inc., 1978. When alternatives at home appear exhausted, when adjustment is overwhelming, this directory could help you locate a private, state or public facility for the emotionally disturbed or socially maladjusted. The schools are often described by the IQ range, or minimums that are acceptable for their students and are organized by states and treatment specialty.

- Dodson, Fitzhugh, *How to Parent.* NY: Signet Books, 1971. Particularly good for new parents, this book (available in paperback) focuses on parenting attitudes and skills regarding the preschool child from newborns up to about age six. It includes excellent summary information about reading materials for young children that focus on their feelings and interpersonal relationships.

- Donahue, Phil, "Gifted Children and Suicide," NBC-TV, Jan. 16, 1981. This 45 minute videotaped program is an excellent tool for increasing community consciousness and awareness of special needs of this often misunderstood minority. The parents of Dallas Egbert and Sean Casey share the hindsights of being parents of gifted children who have committed suicide. Joyce Juntune, executive director of the National Association for Gifted Children, along with others including Dr. James Webb and a highly gifted high school senior, provide further perspectives. A 3/4″ videotape of this program with no commercials is loaned to groups for noncommercial purposes. For information contact: Project SENG, School of Professional Psychology, Wright State University, Dayton, OH 45435.

- Dreikurs, R. and Soltz, V., *Children: The Challenge*. NY: Hawthorne Books, Inc., 1964. Available in paperback and hardcover, this is a "must" book! It offers the basic principles and techniques for encouraging a responsible child. Parents are advised to let "natural consequences" occur wherever possible, rather than to impose artificial consequences. Conveying a sense of trust, adequacy, and personal responsibility for one's own actions are key dimensions in raising children. Numerous examples of creative, good sense solutions to common child-rearing problems are provided, and you will see yourself and your children in this book many times. The major problem with Dreikurs is that sometimes parents feel guilty because his suggestions seem so "obvious" once you read about them. You must remember that Dreikurs and Soltz are writing this in the quiet of their study, and that it is a composite of their best ideas. So do not feel guilty, but do try to incorporate a lot of their principles in your parenting.

- Dreyer, Sharon, Spredemann, *The Bookfinder: A Guide to Children's Literature About the Needs and Problems of Youth Aged 2-15*. Circle Pines, MN: American Guidance Service,

1977. You will find this reference book to be invaluable for directing children to books that focus on numerous and diverse problems of growing up. Over 1,000 worthwhile children's books are catalogued, each of which allows the child to personally identify with book characters in ways that provide insight. Each book is readily indexed according to the topic and feelings exemplified in the story, and each book's content is summarized, along with the age range of children who would be most likely to enjoy the book. Each topic is also listed within an index category, thus allowing a cross-reference to the listing of relevant books and age ranges.

- Ehrlich, V. *Gifted Children: A Guide for Parents and Teachers.* Englewood Cliffs, NJ: Prentice Hall, 1982. The author's experiences with the Astor schools in New York provide her with an excellent background and understanding. This book touches on many areas of concern to parents of gifted children, and gives many practical suggestions for parents to help them work within the school settings.

- Einstein, Elizabeth, *The Stepfamily: Living, Loving and Learning.* NY: Macmillan, 1982. Though not written specifically about gifted children, this book provides important guidelines and information in an era when remarriage is quite commonplace, and as children and adults struggle with creating a stepfamily. This book can be particularly helpful for families whose children are pre-teens.

- ERIC Clearinghouse on Handicapped and Gifted Children: 1920 Association Drive; Reston, VA 22091. Provides computerized search and summary print-outs from extensive research studies.

- Feldhusen, John (Ed.), *Toward Excellence in Gifted Education.* Denver: Love Publishing Co., 1985. An outstanding primer on gifted education, this book highlights and discusses most of the key issues in gifted education, as well as explaining clearly and succinctly the terms and concepts that often confuse parents — such as "scope and sequence" and "program articulation." This book may improve parents' interactions with school gifted programs, as well as greatly helping schools that are beginning to establish programs for their gifted students.

- Fox, Lynn H., Identification of the Academically Gifted. *American Psychologist,* 1981, Vol. 36, No. 10, 1103-1111. Included as part of a special issue by the American Psychological Association, this article reviews the various criteria that scientists and public officials have used for identifying the academically gifted. Fox notes limitations of these, and recommends additional measures that seem more appropriate, particularly with persons from disadvantaged populations.

- Galbraith, Judy, *The Gifted Kids' Survival Guide (For Ages 11-18).* Minneapolis: Free Spirit Publishing Co., 1983.

- Galbraith, Judy, *The Gifted Kids' Survival Guide (For Ages 10 and Under).* Minneapolis: Free Spirit Publishing Co., 1984. These books are written *for,* not just *about,* smart, creative, gifted kids. They answer many of the questions such kids raise about themselves, their relationships, and their thinking styles. They give practical advice to handling situations like "How can you make school more interesting, more challenging?" or "How can I handle kids who tease me about being smart?"

- Gallagher, James J. (Ed.), *Gifted Children: Reaching Their Potential.* NY: Trillium Press, 1979. The 25 chapters in this book were selected from presentations at the Second World Conference on Gifted Children held in 1977. In addition to the major speeches made at the conference, other chapters include research and discussion on curriculum proposals, facilitative environments for fostering giftedness and creativity, research on program effectiveness, theoretical reconceptualizations about education, and studies on families of gifted children. Although some parts may be difficult reading for the layperson, much of the book can be understood by the average parent of a gifted child.

- Gardner, Howard, *Frames of Mind: The Theory of Multiple Intelligences.* New York: Basic Books, 1983. This book is what it says it is — a discussion of Gardner's theories about intelligence, and some very important reconceptualizations. Because he differs from many other voices in research on intelligence and intelligence testing, it is helpful to be familiar with these ideas about the several intelligences he describes. These include: linguistic, musical, logical-mathematical, spatial, bodily-kinesthetic, interpersonal, and intrapersonal. Two other books of his, *Artful Scribbles: The Significance of Children's Drawings* and *Art, Mind and Brain: A Cognitive Approach to Creativity* are also of interest.

- Ginott, Haim, *Between Parent and Child.* NY: Macmillan, 1965. Focusing on feelings, this book is important basic reading for parents whose children are age two or older. Key points include not taking literally everything the child says, but instead listening for the meaning behind the words. He also discusses recognizing feelings, helping the child develop accurate labels for feelings, distinguishing between feelings and behaviors, setting limits, and giving choices. He makes the fundamentals warm and alive, and gives techniques for expressing feelings while still maintaining dignity for those involved.

- Ginott, Haim, *Between Parent and Teenager.* NY: Macmillan, 1969. A sequel to *Between Parent and Child,* this book offers sound basic advice and understanding for this often puzzling time. The focus continues to be on understanding feelings and giving choices, while simultaneously setting enforceable limits. Communication areas are also addressed.

- George, William C.; Cohn, Sanford J. and Stanley, Julian C. (Eds.), *Educating the Gifted, Acceleration and Enrichment.*

Baltimore: The Johns Hopkins University Press, 1979. This book presents a balanced symposium on the relative merits of acceleration and enrichment. In comparing acceleration to lockstep educational methods, its conclusions strongly favor acceleration, including radical acceleration, for the highly gifted child who wishes to move ahead.

- Greenfield, Patricia Marks, *Mind and Media*. Cambridge, MA: Harvard University Press, 1984. A research-oriented look at the advantages (and dangers) of television, video games and computers. This fascinating and enlightening book offers suggestions for methods of using the new media in ways that will limit their destructive potential and enhance their genuine value. Parents and teachers need to examine their assumptions about the primacy of traditional academic methods and of reading in the education of children. Particularly valuable for those parents whose impulse is to ban television viewing altogether.

- Grost, Audrey, *Genius in Residence*. Englewood Cliffs, NJ: Prentice-Hall, 1970. This book is a must for anyone with an exceptionally gifted child or anyone who wants to know more about the highest ranges of intellectual possibility. Audrey Grost details life with her son, Mike, with style, wit and flair. From his attempt to explain Picasso's blue period to another child on their first day in kindergarten to his early days as a ten year old college student, we follow Mike and his family in their quest to let Mike live a life that was "normal" for a child with one of the finest minds of his generation.

- Haensly, Patricia A. and Nash, William R., *Mountains to Climb*. St. Paul, MN: National Association for Gifted Children, 1984. A book for the pre-teen or adolescent gifted youngster, that discusses such options as enrichment and acceleration, as well as types of resources available in various metropolitan and rural areas. The book offers suggestions directly to gifted and talented youth about how *they* can locate resources and opportunities to aid their intellectual and creative development.

- Hollingsworth, L.S., *Children Above 180 I.Q.* NY: Arno Press, 1975. (Reprint of 1943 edition). During the early years of use of the Stanford-Binet Intelligence Scale, several children were identified with IQ scores of 180 and above. This book summarizes findings about them in an easily readable, though sometimes quaint, fashion. Hollingsworth's insights generally are as valid today as they were then, and constitute one of the few references on extremely gifted children.

- Horowitz, Frances Degen and O'Brien, Marion, *The Gifted and Talented: Developmental Perspectives.* Washington, D.C.: American Psychological Association, 1985. Encouraged by the American Psychological Association, this book is intended to summarize the professional psychological knowledge concerning gifted and talented. This book deals with conceptual issues, historical trends, and research summaries concerning a wide range of aspects of gifted and talented.

- Hunt, Morton, *The Universe Within.* New York: Simon & Schuster, 1982. Fascinating exploration of the human brain based in part on recent research, but including a history of the study of the mind and intellect.

- Kerr, Barbara, *Smart Girls, Gifted Women.* Columbus, OH: Ohio Psychology Publishing Co., 1985. Warm and real and researched, the book offers compassion and guidance for gifted females and those who care about them. Brief biographies of eminent women are included. Chapter summaries, bibliographies and an appendix of questions and answers contribute to making this an important resource for understanding and nurturing gifted girls.

- Kramer, Alan K. (Ed.), *Gifted Children, Challenging Their Potential: New Perspectives and Alternatives.* NY: Trillium Press, 1981. Published for the World Council for Gifted and

Talented Children, this book contains over 30 articles selected from presentations and workshops delivered at the Third International Conference on Gifted and Talented Children held in Jerusalem in July, 1979. Though most of the articles are written in scholarly fashion for researchers and educators, most can nonetheless be read profitably by knowledgeable parents. Major areas include different approaches to defining giftedness, methods of nurturing giftedness, curriculum alternatives, counseling and family characteristics, and cultural influences on gifted children.

- Kuralt, Charles, "Gifted Children," CBS-TV Sunday Morning News, February 2, 1982. This 15 minute videotape excerpt focuses on a family with several gifted children as they cope with everyday life, as they think about giftedness, and as they participate in a parents' group. A 3/4" videotape of this program with no commercials is available for loan to groups for noncommercial purposes. For information contact: Project SENG, School of Professional Psychology, Wright State University, Dayton, OH 45435 (513-293-5225).

- Laubensfels, Jean, *The Gifted Student, An Annotated Bibliography.* Westport, CT: Greenwood Press, 1977. Hundreds of articles and books with a detailed index to help you locate research results and expert analyses regarding the gifted student.

- Lewis, David, *How to Be a Gifted Parent.* NY: Norton, 1981. Offers practical principles and constructive concepts designed to cultivate curiosity and confidence. Dr. Lewis primarily speaks to parents of children from pregnancy to five years. He emphasizes the value of assisting children to work through problems. Also included are techniques for meeting the special stressful needs of parents of these preschool gifted children! Thank you, Dr. Lewis, we appreciate your empathy and encouragement.

- Maccoby, Eleanor E., *Social Development: Psychological Growth in the Parent-Child Relationship*. NY: Harcourt-Brace-Jovanovich, 1980. This is a basic source for guiding a child's social development. It gives a perspective on parenting techniques and the resulting expected child behaviors. It is clearly written with summary sections that provide valuable reference for such issues as a child's aggression, attachment relationships, sex typing, and moral development.

- Miller, Alice, *Prisoners of Childhood*. NY: Basic Books Inc., 1981. This book promotes important insights for parents about the child's view of the world. It is worthwhile reading to absorb awareness about how parents may inadvertently be inhibiting a child's emotional, intellectual, and pragmatic development. Gifted parents may drift into conveying that their child only feels loved when he is accomplishing and is becoming more of what his parents, themselves, wanted to be.

- Miller, B.S. and Price, M. (Eds.), *The Gifted Child, the Family and the Community*. NY: Walker and Company and the American Association for Gifted Children, 1981. This potpourri contains thirty-three brief but wide-ranging essays that provide a quick overview of the gifted child. Written for lay persons, this book would serve as a good general introduction to the field and can whet an appetite for more information. Few topics, however, are presented in depth, although some unusual areas are included such as a business perspective on the gifted.

- Moore, Linda Perigo, *Does This Mean My Kid's a Genius?* NY: McGraw-Hill Book Company, 1981. Linda Moore evidences having been there as she shares her joys, exasperations, humorous observations and survival tactics for parenting a GC. These include: How to talk to your GC with more impact than background noise; the fear of going public with your news of identification; where you can go for help; and T.V. It's so delightfully discussed that you'll feel that you already have an ally!

- Patterson, G. and Guillion, E., *Living with Children: New Methods for Parents and Teachers*. Chicago: Research Press, 1968. This unusual book focuses on psychological principles of sharing behavior through behavior modification use of reinforcement. It is presented in a paperback, programmed book form which may take a little getting used to. Even so, it is very helpful for parents or teachers who need to help others (or themselves) modify their behavior. The focus of the book is on behavior and the overt expressions of emotions. Little is said about the child's feelings inside.

- Rimm, Sylvia, *Underachievement Syndrome: Causes and Cures*. Watertown, WI: Apple Publishing Co., 1986. A helpful, often entertaining, book about a serious problem. A great deal of practical advice is contained here, particularly about family patterns that promote or maintain underachievement.

- Strang, Ruth, *Helping Your Gifted Child*. NY: E.P. Dutton, 1960. Written primarily for parents, this comprehensive book includes behavior characteristics of gifted children from preschool through adolescence. Pertinent case studies illustrate suggested means to positively develop a gifted child's unique abilities in cooperative ways at home and at school.

- Tannenbaum, A.J. and Newman, E., *Somewhere to Turn: Strategies for Parents of Gifted and Talented Children*. NY: Teachers College Press, Columbia University, 1980. Though much attention, perhaps too much, is given to forming parent advocacy groups, substantial information is included that is directly relevant to parenting gifted children. Intellectual enrichment and emotional development techniques are included, though only about 25 to 30 pages are devoted to these techniques and approaches. The advocacy portion is quite worthwhile.

- Torrance, E. Paul, *Gifted Children in the Classroom*. NY: Mac-Millan Publishing Co., Inc., 1965. This book is a primer to help readers start learning principles about gifted children, including why bother, identification, motivation, ideal and actual values of teachers, and much more to help you become an advocate for your child.
- Torrance, E. Paul, *Guiding Creative Talent*. Englewood Cliffs: Prentice Hall, 1962. This valuable source of support and enlightenment contains many whimsical and actual case illustrations. These examples, combined with principles from his research, help the reader to know, accept and nurture the creatively gifted child.
- Vail, Priscilla L., *The World of the Gifted Child*. NY: Walker and Company, 1979 and New York: Penguin, 1980 (paperback). She could become one of your friends! There are stories of warm, real people exemplifying many typical situations. She suggests means of coping that help parents feel more adequate in their sometimes awesome role. Geared more to attributes than to ages, Vail suggests extensive imaginative activities and materials for our special children that may be more an investment of time and creative thinking than of money. Lots of warm fuzzies in this guide to helping gifted children meet their own needs!
- Whitmore, Joanne Rand, *Giftedness, Conflict and Underachievement*. Rockleigh, NJ: Allyn and Bacon, Inc., 1980. Designed as a college text, this book integrates the educational, social and emotional development of gifted children with a specific program for underachievers. This perspective provides extensive awareness and practical techniques to promote positive self-concept.
- Willings, David, *The Creatively Gifted*. Cambridge, England: Woodhead-Faulkner, 1980 (Available through Ohio Psychology Publishing Co., 131 N. High Street, Columbus, OH

43215). Another important book, particularly for adolescent or adult gifted. Willings's case studies and especially his delineation of "adaptive," "elaborative" and "developmental" thinking are well worth the effort that may be involved in locating this book.

- Witty, Paul (Ed.), *The Gifted Child*. Boston: Heath and Co., 1951. This book, published for the American Association for Gifted Children, provides a good background context for understanding today's gifted programming. Witty's book demonstrates the cyclical concern for gifted, and how educational and governmental support has waxed and waned.
- Wright, Logan, Ph.D., *Parent Power, A Guide to Responsible Child Rearing*. NY: William Morrow and Co., Inc., 1980. Rewards for your time with Dr. Logan Wright are multiple. Delightfully intimate and entertaining, this book describes in practical and clear fashion professionally proven principles to portray the power parents have to enhance their children. Parent power is the catalyst for encouragement, love, trust, worth and responsibility. You will love letting Dr. Wright tell you how to generate these joys.

"New opinions are always suspected, and usually opposed, without any other reason but because they are not already common."

John Locke

"Thought is the blossom; language the bud; action the fruit behind it."

Ralph Waldo Emerson

"The hallmark of our age is the tension between related aspirations and sluggish institutions."

John Gardner

"We can lick gravity, but sometimes the paperwork is overwhelming."

Wernher von Braun

"That is true culture which helps us to work for the social betterment of all."

Henry Ward Beecher

CHAPTER XV

ASSOCIATIONS AND ADVOCACY GROUPS FOR GIFTED CHILDREN

- American Association for Gifted Children/Talent Identification
  Program
  Duke University TIP
  1121 West Main Street, Suite 100
  Durham, NC 27701
  (919) 683-1400 • FAX (919) 683-1741
  webpage: http://www.jayi.com/tip
- American Mensa, Ltd.201 Main Street, Suite 201
  Fort Worth, TX 76102-3115
  (817) 332-2600
  e-mail: ammensa@onramp.net • webpage: http://www.us.mensa.org
- The Association for the Gifted (TAG)
  Council for Exceptional Children
  1920 Association Drive
  Reston, VA 22091
  (800-328-0272)
  webpage: http://www.cec.sped.org/eric.html
- Center for Academic Precocity
  College of Education
  Arizona State University
  Box 872711
  Tempe, AZ 85287-1711
  (602) 965-4757 • FAX (602) 965-1069
  e-mail: cap@asu.edu • webpage: http://www.cap.ed.asu.edu/

- Center for Talented Youth (CTY)
  Institute for the Academic Advancement of Youth (IAAY)
  Johns Hopkins University
  Charles and 34th Streets
  Baltimore, MD 21218
  (410) 516-0337
  webpage: http://www.jhu.edu/~gifted/
- Center for Talent Development
  Northwestern University
  617 Dartmouth Place
  Evanston, IL 60208
  (708) 491-3782
  webpage: http://www.ctdnet.acns.nwu.edu
- Council of State Directors of Programs for the Gifted
  c/o Michael Hall, Specialist
  Office of Public Instruction
  Montana Department of Education
  P.O. Box 202501
  Helena, MT 59620-2501
  (406) 444-4422
  webpage: http://www.netc.org/web_mod/gifted_ed/
- The Gifted Child Society
  190 Rock Road
  Glen Rock, NJ 07452-1736
  (201) 444-6530
  webpage: http://www.gifted.org/society/society.html
- Gifted Development Center
  777 Pearl Street
  Denver, CO 80303
  (303) 837-8378 FAX (303) 831-7465
  e-mail: gifted@gifteddevelopmentcenter.com
  webpage: www.gifteddevelopmentcenter.com
- Hollingworth Center for Highly Gifted Children
  827 Central Avenue, #282
  Dover, NH 03820-2506
  (207) 655-3767 or (508) 597-0977

- National Association for Gifted Children (NAGC)
  1707 L Street, NW, Suite 550
  Washington, DC 20036
  (202) 785-4268
  webpage: http://www.nagc.org
- National Research Center on the Gifted and Talented
  The University of Connecticut
  362 Fairfield Road, U-7
  Storrs, CT 06269-2007
  (203) 486-4826
  webpage: http://www.ucc.uconn.edu/~wwwgt/nrcgt.html
- Rocky Mountain Talent Search
  2135 E. Wesley Avenue
  200 Wesley Hall
  University of Denver
  Denver, CO 80208
  (303) 871-2983
- Supporting Emotional Needs of Gifted (SENG)
  405 White Hall
  P.O. Box 5190
  Kent State University
  Kent, OH 44242
  (330) 672-4450 • Fax: (330) 672-2512
  e-mail: SENG@amethyst.educ.kent.edu
  webpage: http://educ.kent.edu/Frames/EFSS/SENG/mission.html
- The World Council for Gifted and Talented Children, Inc.
  18401 Hiawatha Street
  Northridge CA 91326
  (818) 368-7501 FAX 818-368-2163
  email: worldgt@earthlink.net

CANADA

- Association for Bright Children
  19 Sherwood Drive
  Kingston, Ontario CANADA K&M 2E2
  (613) 544-9585
  webpage: http://www.fcbe.edu.on.ca/SEAC/abchome.html

INDEX